• • • • •

# WINNING
## THE
# DIVORCE
# WAR

BY
## RONALD FARRINGTON SHARP
### ATTORNEY-AT-LAW

ALLWORTH PRESS
NEW YORK

04   03   02   01   00   99   98        5   4   3   2   1

Published by Allworth Press
An imprint of Allworth Communications
10 East 23rd Street, New York NY 10010

Cover design by Douglas Design Associates, New York, NY

Page composition/typography by SR Desktop Services, Ridge, NY

ISBN: 1-58115-009-1

Library of Congress Catalog Card Number: 98-72759


Printed in Canada

# CONTENTS

# INTRODUCTION

**G**etting married is a gamble. The National Center for Health Statistics reports that 50 percent of all marriages now end in divorce. While that figure is down slightly from the all-time high of 56 percent in 1979, a couple getting married today still has only a fifty-fifty chance of having a successful marriage. Not a great bet by anybody's standards. Divorce has become an established fact of American life, and marriage is coming to be thought of as something less than a lifetime commitment. No longer is the so-called nuclear family of father, mother, and children the norm.

Occasionally, amicable divorces do occur, the couple shaking hands and wishing each other the best as they begin their separate lives. Unfortunately, the friendly and reasonable divorce is the exception. Typically, emotions run high and there are numerous points of contention. Sometimes one partner, acting from need, greed, or merely a desire to punish the other partner, will try to grab all the marbles.

It is important that anyone contemplating a divorce knows the law as well as specific strategies that will safeguard his or her rights to marital property, child support, child custody, and alimony. Antenuptial agreements (also called prenuptial and premarital agreements) are discussed and suggestions are given on how to increase the odds of their enforcement. Specific suggestions on actions you can take now to improve your position in a future divorce are presented. The sad fact is that the one you love today may be your most hated enemy tomorrow.

For those who are in the middle of a divorce, this manual will tell you how to present yourself in the best possible light. Whether you like it or not, you are already involved in an adversarial process and must therefore use all legal means possible to achieve the best result. Forget mother's admonishment to "be nice." In the pages that follow, I will reveal certain dirty tricks that your spouse may try to pull on you. Thwarting just one of these will make reading this book worthwhile. Knowledge is power.

If your divorce is already over, there is information that can help you modify certain parts of the divorce judgment. A final divorce judgment is not always final, particularly when children are involved.

Planning and preparation are the primary notes I will sound over and over on the following pages. Rather than blindly turning your life and future over to a lawyer, you will see how to prepare your case so that your lawyer cannot help but win it. I have heard this maxim often repeated among divorce lawyers: "The one with the best records wins." You will learn how to preserve the important evidence that will later be used by the divorce court to make its decisions. Proper preparation can make a case settle quickly and favorably, where it would otherwise have gone to trial.

Nonlegal, not illegal, strategies will be discussed to position you in an advantageous legal position relative to your spouse. For example, you will be told how to get the best lawyer for yourself and how to narrow your spouse's choice of attorneys. Special attention should be paid to chapter 5, "Cease-Fire: The Enforceable Separation Agreement." This infrequently used but powerful special strategy can make your divorce case slide smoothly through the courts on your terms, sometimes even over the objections of your spouse.

The terminology is as gender-neutral as possible. All the examples, case studies, and strategies are equally applicable to either sex, and I have tried to balance the use of "he" and "she" throughout the text.

Warning: This is not a textbook and it is not intended as legal advice. There are exceptions to every rule and each state, and sometimes even each court within a state has its own peculiarities. What *Winning the Divorce War* can do is give you some insight into practical ways others have handled situations you may face yourself. You might call it a damage-control book—ways to be sure that you are not taken advantage of and that you get what you want and deserve. This information is based on the thousands of divorce cases I have handled and advised on over the nearly twenty-three years I have practiced family law.

Second Warning: This is not a book on dealing with the emotional trauma of the divorce and separation process. There are plenty of books written by those in the social sciences to help you handle the sociopsychological aspects of the breakup of your marriage. You will not find any advice on how to cope here. However, it has been my experience that those who go through the divorce process in a position of strength, with proper preparation and clearly defined goals, suffer far less stress and anxiety than those who leave everything to their lawyers.

In the appendixes, I have suggested resources including some of what is available on the Internet. This is a battle manual, an easy-to-read reference book using a war analogy to bring home to the reader the serious nature of the adversary court process. I do not recommend or endorse every tactic and strategy outlined in the following pages, but reveal them in the spirit of the free flow of information since they may well be used against you by your spouse. Courts operate primarily on objective evidence—they can make decisions based only upon what they are shown. Therefore, you must show the court why you should get what you want and give good reasons for such a decision. Knowing what you want, what you can get, and how to get it are the themes of this book.

# CHAPTER ONE

# THE PREEMPTIVE STRIKE: PLANNING FOR THE DIVORCE TO COME

Sharon arrived early for her appointment. She was nervous as she was shown into my office. This was the first time she had ever been to a lawyer.

"I didn't even know our marriage was in trouble," she said, tears forming in the corners of her eyes. "I came home from work and his stuff was gone—along with a lot of the furniture. He cleaned out the bank accounts and took one of the cars, the one that's paid for. What can I do?"

Before I could answer, she added, "And the kids. He took both of them along with their stuff."

I cleared my throat to respond and she pulled a sheaf of folded papers from her purse, holding them out to me.

"And yesterday a man came and gave me these." I took the papers while she searched in her purse for a tissue.

The divorce papers. I scanned them quickly. They were the typical fill-in-the-blank forms asking for a divorce and court orders giving him temporary custody, ordering her to pay child support, and putting a freeze on her disposing of any marital assets.

She waited expectantly for me to tell her how I would miraculously solve her problems.

It would not be easy.

Nor cheap.

Her husband must have read my book.

Of course something could be done for Sharon, given a competent lawyer, plenty of money, lots of time and a heavy dose of fortitude. She did not have to be in this position.

After giving her ten minutes to tell me how she felt about the situation, I picked up my pad and started running down the normal list of questions I use to evaluate a case like hers. I was disappointed but not surprised by her answers. No, she did not know for sure how much money he made. She was never given any money and did not have access to the checkbook. Her husband, Bob, left cash in a drawer in the bedroom and she went there when she needed money. No, she couldn't give me a list of assets and their values. She knew some of the things that they owned, of course, but had no idea if they were paid for, financed, or leased. She did not even know where the deeds to the property or tax returns were kept, whether he had a pension or profit-sharing plan, or even if they had any savings. Bob took care of all that.

He sure did.

The court orders were all perfectly legal and enforceable until the judge ruled otherwise. All Bob had to do was ask for them and the court automatically gave him what he wanted. It was now up to her to try and change them—if that was her wish. The court assumes that she consents if she does not object. If Sharon had not come to see me (and a surprisingly large number of people do nothing at all when served with papers), her husband would have gotten away with everything. As it was, he had her on the ropes before the fight even started.

Sharon was not an exceptional case. Most divorce litigants are so distraught over their relationship problems that they do not take care of the practical aspects of the separation process. In almost every case, they do not even know what steps to take to protect their own interests. Seeing a lawyer is about all that the majority of people do to help themselves—which should be all you have to do in a perfect world. The sad fact is that the lawyer you choose may or may not be a competent and capable divorce lawyer. Law is analogous to medicine in that certain lawyers have certain areas they consider their specialty. Do you really want a bankruptcy expert handling your divorce case? Most general practice attorneys handle a wide variety of case types and cannot possibly be expert in each of them. However, even a general practice lawyer can do a very good job in a divorce if the client is well prepared. Certain states certify attorneys as divorce specialists, but this is no guarantee of great representation.

In the final analysis, the lawyer is only as good as the ammunition you provide. Do not turn your entire present and future over to someone who may or may not know what he is doing or care what happens to you.

Wake up! There are numerous practical steps following that you can take to improve the outcome of your divorce case. And there's a bonus: just by reading this book, you will suffer less anxiety over the divorce process because it will no longer be a mystery. If you go so far as to take action on a few of my suggestions, both your confidence will increase and your status in the legal process will improve. Remember what Francis Bacon said: "Knowledge itself is power."

Try to be more like Bob and less like Sharon. In other words, control the situation rather than be controlled by it. You do this by acquiring knowledge and by taking action to protect your interests.

## Know Your Enemy

To maintain objectivity, you must consider your spouse the enemy. If you were at war and wanted to win, you would have to know your enemy's strengths and weaknesses. You would keep track of his troop deployments, know the extent of his land and air forces, and analyze the politics in his country. So it is with a contested court action. It is called the adversary system because you and your spouse are adversaries—enemies, if you will. It is sometimes hard to consider your spouse the enemy, but you must. Sure, you were both madly in love once upon a time. Maybe *you* still are. Perhaps you both will be again. But the sad, cold fact is that whatever your spouse gets in a divorce is something that you give up. Being generous in a divorce settlement is not going to bring him or her back. Nor will it make up for leaving your spouse. Guilt is usually temporary and often misplaced. Do not give everything up to ease your conscience if you are the one who is leaving the marriage. You may regret it later. Amiable divorces do happen, but not often. Your spouse is not looking out for your best interests.

## Keep Records

Knowing your enemy means being fully informed as to your spouse's past and present personal and financial picture. Look at the following chart. Make sure you are able to provide this information on your spouse either from memory or from records and paperwork available to you. The information listed can be extremely valuable to your attorney in a divorce case.

---

### SPOUSE INFORMATION

Full legal name

Date of birth

Social security number

Driver's license number

Education: where spouse attended high school, college, trade or professional school, dates attended, degrees

Job history: employers, job titles, rates of pay, promotions

Income: from employment, investments, rents, royalties, cash income, "side jobs"

Fringe benefits: retirement plans, Keogh plans, 401(k)s, profit sharing, stock option plans, insurance, accrued vacation or sick leave, severance pay, employment contract benefits

Criminal history: all arrests and convictions, even for traffic offenses

Alcohol and drug use history: particularly if such use has led to personal or family problems

Emotional or psychiatric history

Past "fault" indiscretions: dates, names, and places of incidents of adultery, cruelty, desertion, etc.

---

I don't mean to imply that you should have an actual file folder on your spouse. As a practical matter, we all know that if your spouse found such a dossier, it would create a very uncomfortable situation for you. But your spouse does not have to know about it. If you never need to use the information, then that is terrific. Try to be like a librarian—if you don't know all the answers, at least know where to find them.

This all sounds very cold and calculating, but it is simply a matter of being prepared. Even leaving aside the question of divorce, these are things you have a right to know, and should know, about your spouse.

## Control the Purse Strings

The flip side to knowing a great deal about your spouse is to keep your spouse from knowing a great deal about you. In no area is this more useful than in your finances. Keep your spouse in the dark. Offer to assume the burden of paying the bills, writing checks, and doing the taxes. Your spouse will be happy that you have made life easier by taking over these mundane tasks. At the very least, you will then have access to all the financial information. Knowing what is there is most of the way toward assuring that you get your fair share. Of course, if it prevents your spouse from having a clear picture of the family finances, that is also to your advantage. If you control the money and records, you have another weapon in your growing arsenal. A good lawyer can find out a lot of information about your spouse for you, but the so-called discovery process in court can be very time consuming and costly.

## Get It in Your Name

An interesting facet of the law in Mississippi is that the property in a divorce case goes to whoever's name it is titled in. So, if you marry a man who owns a house in Mississippi, it would be a good idea if you talked him into selling it and buying another one. Just for the two of you, with your name on it as his wife. It is even better if you can arrange to have some of the money from selling the old one put into other assets— such as a new car for you. You don't live in Mississippi? The same advice holds true.

In short-term marriages in particular, judges like to put the parties back in the positions they were in before they married—sort of a "no-harm, no-foul" policy. If you and your spouse dispose of the things you owned before the marriage and later commingled the assets into new ones, it may be difficult or impossible to distinguish which were the old assets and which are new ones. Therefore, all the assets may be split.

In the nine community property states, of course, all property is considered jointly owned regardless of who owns it. However, in the other "equity" states, the division between the competing parties is based on any number of factors, including who owned what before the marriage. If the premarital assets still exist or can be traced directly to new assets, then the court may well award those to the party who brought them into the marriage.

When you buy anything of major value during the marriage, get it either in your name alone or jointly with your spouse. If you are buying something and want it in just your name, tell your spouse something like this: "I heard that if you get sued, they can take away things that are in both names."

If your spouse wants something in just his name, you could say: "I read that if you have things in separate names and then you die that you get tied up in probate for years, but joint ownership avoids probate and all the lawyers."

Everybody wants to avoid lawyers. The above statements are generally true, though there are some exceptions, but does your spouse know the exceptions? Probably not. Be assertive. The point is that if it is in your name, your spouse cannot get rid of it or hide it without your consent. At least it's less likely.

## Be Ready for the Custody Case

In most states custody goes to—no, not necessarily the mother—the one who the judge thinks has been more responsible for the children's care in the past and who is more capable of caring for them in the future, and the one with whom the children will be better off. It does not read that way in any law book, but that's what it always comes down to. When you go into court to have the judge decide custody, you must present the best case possible. You cannot undo the past, but you can prepare for the future. Be prepared to show the judge how you have gone out of your way to nurture and care for your children. Give him tangible proof that the children look to you for their care. Proof is best made by specific examples. For instance, you are the one who takes the children to the doctor, arranges their birthday parties, attends parent-teacher conferences, drives them to the movies, and gives permission for sleepovers. Let the judge hear other people who should know tell him about the high quality of your care and concern for the children. The judge must see things as you do. Chapter 3 covers the preparation of a custody plan in detail.

Most important of all is to keep records. Write down the names of potential witnesses. Record the times you did things with the kids. As Raoul Felder, a top divorce lawyer, put it in an interview, "I say the one who keeps the best records carries the day." If nothing else, write things on the wall calendar and save the calendars.

## Prepare for the Support/Alimony Case

Alimony is financial support for the spouse and is awarded when the spouse has no income or much less income than her partner and needs help to maintain a standard of living close to that she enjoyed while married. Alimony can be awarded in two ways: either you and your spouse agree on it or the court orders it after a trial. If the court orders it, a number of factors will be considered. These include, primarily, the history of the marriage, the age, health, and earning abilities of each partner, the amount of property awarded to each, and the needs and prior standard of living of each partner.

As a wife, remember that you will not get permanent alimony if the court thinks you do a fine job of taking care of yourself. Sometimes the woman who never worked is better off than the working wife. She can get maximum alimony and still start a career after the divorce doing something she likes, with a financial cushion on which to rest. She also may have a stronger custody case since she can be with the children more than the working mother can.

Of course, this advice is not always practical. Sometimes economics dictate that both spouses work. And a woman with a strongly established career is better off financially than the one who does not work but receives alimony. If you were approaching the question merely from the standpoint of how to maximize the chance of getting alimony, not working would be a step in the right direction.

Watch out for lawyers who tell you there is no alimony in your state (unless you live in Texas, where that literally is the case). Sometimes, a lawyer will use semantics to discourage you from asserting your rights, either because he is unskilled or is interested in a quick uncontested case with no complications. The term "alimony" has been replaced in many jurisdictions by the term "spousal support." It is the same thing and even if not regularly awarded, it is still something for which you can ask.

There is also something called "temporary alimony." The spouse who earns substantially less can often get alimony for a few months or years even if he or she does not qualify for permanent alimony payments. It is fairly easy for the lesser-income spouse to qualify for temporary alimony until he or she is reestablished financially.

As a husband, remember that child support ends someday. Alimony can be forever. If your wife is dependent upon you, the court may make you continue to pay. Get her a job. Send her to school. Get her some kind of marketable skill so that you can show the judge how she could take care of herself. If you are the one asking for alimony and are not now working, bring in an employment expert or physician or both to testify as to your health and earning ability.

In addition, child support schedules often factor in the custodial parent's income in determining support levels; so if you plan on giving her physical custody of the kids, remember that you can reduce your support obligation if she's working. If you must pay alimony, be sure that there is a provision in your order that it terminate forever upon your wife's remarriage or when she begins to cohabit with another person. If she has assumed another marital-like relationship, the dependency upon you should end. Also ask your lawyer about the deductibility of alimony payments and the possibility of lump-sum alimony. Generally, alimony payments are deductible to the payer and taxable to the receiver. This is an important consideration when alimony is a part of your total settlement package.

Remember that alimony is not for wives alone. Nowadays the laws are written to treat both sexes equally. Husbands can now sometimes get alimony if the wife is the one with the higher income.

Note: In some jurisdictions the person who is at fault in the divorce cannot collect alimony. Ask your lawyer about the law in your state. For instance, proving adultery on the part of your spouse may defeat an alimony claim. In seventeen states, so-called marital misconduct can affect whether alimony is awarded at all and, if so, how much. Fault, then, can be a factor in awarding alimony even if the decision as to whether or not a divorce is granted is not based on fault. To properly evaluate your case, your attorney must have all information about the past relationship of you and your spouse. Do not hide anything from your lawyer.

## Adopting Your Spouse's Children

Adoption puts the new parent in place of the old. This includes rights, such as the right to inherit from the new parent, and duties, such as the new parent's duty to support the child. If you get a divorce, it remains your duty to support the adopted child until the age of majority. This can include paying for expensive medical care and even a college education. Know what you are getting into before you agree.

Conversely, if you are the one with the children, encourage your spouse to adopt them. A mother whose child has a father who does not pay support or has disappeared can get another shot at child support if her new husband adopts the children. He may also think twice about filing for divorce later on if he knows he will be on the hook for support. But remember that you may also be giving your spouse a legal ground to ask for custody of the adopted child.

If you are the one giving up the rights to your children, be aware that you are not automatically eliminating any support arrearages. The child support you owed will still be owing.

## Premarital Agreements

These are also called prenuptial or antenuptial contracts. If you have a lot and your spouse does not, get one before you get married. They are almost universally becoming recognized by the law as enforceable. Go to a lawyer so that it is done properly (see chapter 8). Even if they are not legally recognized in your state right now, they might be later or you might move somewhere in the future where they are legally enforceable. Even if the contract is not legally binding, it serves another purpose. Just like the meaningless signs in parking garages that say "Not Responsible for Damage to Cars," your spouse may not know the agreement is unenforceable now and therefore may not contest the divorce that you start. Perception can be more real than reality itself.

## Think Two Years Ahead

You have just met a new man/woman who is infinitely more charming, understanding, and attentive than the dolt of a spouse you have now. You want a divorce. Think ahead! Do not give your spouse everything just to get out. Remember that as a rule of thumb you can count on getting at least half of all the marital property if you ask for it. Although you can go back to court for a change of custody or an increase or decrease in alimony or support, the property division is final. You may not care now, in the thrill of newly found freedom, but I can guarantee you that in two years you will kick yourself for giving everything away—especially if by then your new love is just a bitter memory.

CHAPTER TWO

# STRATEGY AND TACTICS: DEFINING YOUR GOALS

When clients come to me seeking representation in a divorce, I always ask this question right up front: Accepting the fact that your marriage is over, what do you see as an ideal end result of the divorce proceeding? There have been a few people who had thought through this question before they came to see me, but most do not have a clear picture of what they hope to achieve. Many people are so broken up emotionally over the fact that the relationship has soured that they give no thought to what they want to have happen.

It is dangerously easy to become so enmeshed in the complexity of the legal process that your real objectives are never met. It is vitally important that you know what you really want.

Many of my clients answer quickly, "I just want out," or "I want everything." Occasionally, I even hear, "I want you to nail the bastard to the wall." Invariably, the first answer is not an accurate reflection of what the client really wants. Such an answer comes from emotion rather than from logic. Identifying the true objective takes some careful and practical thinking.

In addition to understanding your own goal, you need to be able to identify what it is your spouse really wants. There can be serious adverse consequences to misunderstanding your opponent's goal. A look at history gives us a good illustration. I am reminded of the story told by a former official of the Jimmy Carter administration about the hostage crisis in

11

Iran. The U.S. foreign policy experts completely misread the objectives and goals of the ayatollah and did not believe him when he told them what he wanted. They wrongly assumed that his stated goal of having the shah's head on a pole was an artifice to cover up his "real" goal. The United States had no intention of turning the shah over to the Iranians. The ayatollah's stated goal was so unrealistic that the United States did not even believe it was his goal. As it turned out, the shah died, making the ayatollah's goal unattainable. Because the United States misread the ayatollah's intentions, the hostages stayed in captivity far longer than would have been necessary. The point is to know your opponent's goal and to make your own goal realistic and realizable.

It is not realistic to expect to get everything. Your spouse, no matter how bad he is, even if he ran off with another woman, taking all the money and leaving you with the starving children, will get something from the judge if he asks for it.

To determine your real goal, it is necessary to take a clear-eyed look at the options.

## List Your Goals

Following is a sample selection of goals; there are certainly others, so you may want to modify this list. On a separate sheet of paper, rank the items in the order of their importance to you. Then, decide how many of these you must have and cannot live without. These are the things you cannot bargain away. Draw a line under these items; this is your bottom line. Next, mark the items you would like, ideally, to have. These are the things you can give up if necessary in your bargaining. You will be left with the list of items you do not want. You may initially ask for some of these as red herrings to give up early in the bargaining process. This will make you look like a person ready and willing to compromise.

1. A quick divorce (In most no-fault states, getting the divorce is a foregone conclusion. Since you do not need "grounds," you do not need to worry about whether your spouse will "give" you a divorce, though he can make getting it troublesome.)

  2. Sole custody of one or more children
  3. Maximum child support/payment by you of the least amount possible
  4. Children's college expenses
  5. Paid medical expenses for the children
  6. Unrestricted, unscheduled visitation or specific scheduled visitation
  7. Alimony (also called spousal support) for yourself or no alimony for your spouse
  8. Removal of your spouse from the marital home
  9. Property division
      a. The marital home/proceeds from its sale
      b. Other real estate/proceeds from its sale
      c. Personal property items (furniture, family heirlooms, etc.)
      d. A share in spouse's pension plan
      e. Something in exchange for the value of spouse's education or professional practice
      f. A share or all of business interests, investments, and accounts
      g. Insurance beneficiary designations on spouse to ensure payment of support even after spouse's death
  10. Revenge

This list is just an example and there are many more items you may see as important goals to achieve. After you have made your prioritized list, cast a cold eye at what you say you must have. Is it what you *really* want? Let's look at an example.

Jim was an air-traffic controller working long hours in a high-stress job. He came to see me with his divorce papers in hand, distraught and hurt because his wife had filed. He said he wanted custody of his three-year-old son and had to have the house. After we talked awhile and his initial agitation passed, it became clear that his real fear was that his wife would take the boy and move to another state, where her mother lived, and he would lose touch with his son. He found no real fault with his wife's behavior in regard to the child and admitted that she was a good mother.

What he really wanted was very liberal visitation and to ensure that the child stayed nearby. The fear that his wife would move turned out to be unfounded since she had a good job and could not easily get other employment. The threat to move turned out to be not serious, but an attempt to scare him. Armed with this knowledge, we negotiated an order for joint custody, specific scheduled visitation, a provision that the child's residence could not be moved from the county, and an even division of property. We avoided a very costly and emotionally draining custody fight and gave both parties what they wanted.

It is important to know specifically what you want so that you are not fighting for an unwanted or unimportant goal.

Having custody of the children is to many people the most important goal of all. Many parents would give up all other aspects of the final settlement just to keep the children with them. Full custody gives the custodian full legal rights to all the decision-making regarding the children. What it turns out most parents really want is to maintain a close and continuing relationship with their children, and this can be accomplished without having full legal custody. Remember that "custody" is a legal term. It is important to distinguish between legal custody and legal possession. If you can get joint custody but full legal possession, you have what you really want.

Some people demand custody and full possession without thinking their real desires through. Do you really want custody? Are you prepared to be the parent who prepares all the meals, washes the clothing, does the shopping, chauffeurs them to lessons and ball practice? Do you want to have to look for a sitter every time you want to go out? Are you prepared to be the one who disciplines them? Or to be the one who takes care of them when they are sick? It is more expensive to have custody. You need a larger house or apartment, you'll have higher utility and food costs, and they'll require clothing and lots of other things. Sure you can sometimes get child support, but you can't always count on collecting it. It is not an easy job and gets worse when they become teenagers.

While many parents believe the rewards of having full possession far outweigh the problems, I have had mothers with custody come back to me several years later asking that custody be changed to the father. It looked to Mom like Dad had the much better arrangement—seeing them every weekend and for a few weeks in the summer. She was always the bad guy who set the rules, while Dad let them do what they wanted. When he got tired of them, he sent them back to her. Custody is a big job. You had better be prepared.

I have had parents without custody tell me that since the divorce they now spend more quality time with their children. Visitation acted as a forced scheduled time for parent-child personal interaction, something that did not exist during the marriage.

What about the marital property? Do you really want the house? It is a truism that the same income that supported one household in the past will now have to support two. Is your income sufficient to cover the costs associated with operating the family home? There are taxes, insurance, mortgage payments, and repairs and maintenance. Maybe you would be better off in another, less expensive place. You could buy it with the cash from your share of the house equity or rent and put your cash in the bank.

One of my clients was very insistent that she get all the wedding presents as part of her property division. She reasoned that since her parents paid for the wedding, the gifts should be hers alone. No matter that his family and friends contributed half of the gifts. Her rationale was based on logic, albeit faulty logic. When I had her provide me with a list of the gifts, she realized that she really had no strong interest in keeping many of the items.

Identifying your true important goals is of utmost importance in achieving a good resolution. If you do not know specifically what you want, you never know when you have achieved it. It may well be that you will be able to arrive at an early agreement with your spouse that will satisfy both of you without having to go through the entire litigation process.

## Keep Your Goals to Yourself

Never tell your spouse your goal—he is your *enemy*. Anything he gets is something you will not get. The American legal system is called the adversary system for good reason. Each side is against the other. There is no joint search for the truth, justice, or equity. There is a winner and a loser in every case that goes to trial. Perhaps court is not the most humane place to decide divorce issues, but so long as it is the primary place, each lawyer will use whatever weapons he has to assure victory for his side. And knowledge of your opponent's most cherished objectives is a potent weapon.

Thus, while you are keeping your goals to yourself, you should do everything you can to try to find out what your spouse really wants. At the very least, you can probably make a pretty good guess. By now you probably know him (or her) better than anyone. Knowing his goal will help you achieve your own.

## Give Your Spouse What He Thinks He Wants

As I have said, most people do not know what they really want and can be fooled into accepting something else. Nora's case is a great example.

Her husband George wanted a divorce. He offered her the marital home, worth $200,000 and paid for, one of the two cars, custody of the children, $100 a week in child support, and agreed to pay the household bills for three months while she looked for work. Nora took the offer, thinking he was being eminently fair. He kept only his car and his business. She did not get a lawyer, thinking that a quick settlement would be easier, and she thought she was getting everything she could want.

Nora came to me five years after the divorce, seeking an increase in support. She still thought the deal was fair until I went over some figures with her. Based on his income, I determined that the court would have ordered $500 a week in child support. George had saved $104,000 in support alone over the past five years! And there were still another seven years to go before the youngest reached age eighteen. She would have gotten half the value of the house anyway, so his giving all of it to her netted her only $100,000. But he kept the business, which was worth $150,000 more than the house! So who got the best deal? She got what he wanted her to have, not what she wanted. Fortunately, we were able to increase the support George would have to pay but could not go back to collect it retroactively for the five previous years. And once the property issues are settled, no modification is legally permitted so she was out of luck there.

George knew Nora. He knew she wanted the kids and the house and so was able to talk her into what she thought was a good deal. And she thanked him for it. Maybe you can make your own sweetheart deal by giving your spouse what he thinks he wants. Be sure that when you make your deal, you get all of what you have to have and as much as you would like to have as you can possibly get.

## Do You Really Want a Divorce?

Before you give a quick answer, consider the fact that there are alternatives that may better serve your interests. Unless you are planning on getting remarried, a legal separation (sometimes called an action for "separate maintenance") might be better for you. A legal separation is very much like a divorce in the procedure involved. Papers are still signed and served on the other side, lawyers are involved, and the case is heard by a judge who enters a final written judgment. In a legal separation you still go to court, you can still get custody and support orders, and you can have an enforceable property settlement, yet you are still legally married. This can be very important as we will see later in this chapter under "Dangers of Divorce."

If you just want the jerk away from you but for religious or other reasons do not believe in divorce, a legal separation can be the answer. Be warned though. By filing for a legal separation, you are starting a court case. In most states a defendant spouse (the other side, the enemy) can ask the court to convert the separation action into a divorce case and there is little you can do about it.

Another alternative is the separation agreement. This is in essence a contract that spells out the terms of the separation. It is not signed by a judge and is not a court case, but if properly drawn up, it can be enforced in a court as a contract if it is violated. The terms can even dictate what will happen in any later divorce proceeding. A separation agreement is a good idea if you know what you want and can get your spouse to go along with it. It is sometimes easier to get your spouse to agree to the separation agreement than it would be to get a divorce settled. It is a very effective and legal way to resolve what might become a sticky case. We will go into this topic in depth in chapter 5.

Another alternative to divorce is to just go your separate ways. Of course you cannot rely on the courts for protective orders or enforcement of agreed-upon divisions of property, and you cannot remarry; however, you won't have to deal with lawyers and courts either. If you have children and want to be sure of maintaining either custody or visitation, this is not a great option. Absent a court order, either parent has the same rights to custody and control of the children. For example, suppose you and your husband have agreed to separate without any legal proceedings. The children are going to live with you in New York while your husband is planning to move to California. If he refuses to return the children to you after visitation with him or if he just takes the children away against your wishes, there is little you can do to stop him. Certainly, you can file a fast action in court for custody and hope that New York will take jurisdiction, but you are not protected by the criminal courts for kidnapping nor by the punitive power of the divorce court to punish him with contempt. He is a parent and has parental rights to possession until these are limited by court order.

## Annulment as a Divorce Alternative

Statutes in some states say that marriage to an "idiot" is automatically invalid and can be annulled. The court needs more than just your opinion, though, so get some proof. Seriously though, sometimes marriages can be annulled, eliminating the need for a divorce. Contrary to popular belief, consummation of the marriage (sexual relations between husband and wife) has little to do with the grounds for an annulment.

Grounds for an annulment in general are marriage by force or fraud, preexisting marriage (bigamy), legal incapacity (too young or mentally incompetent), or physical incapacity to

consent. There are other grounds available in some states.
(Delaware, for instance, allows annulment if you can show
you were "just kidding" and married in jest or on a dare.)

The advantage of annulment is that, if granted, the effect is
to wipe out the marriage. Legally, the marriage never existed.
You can say you have never been married, which, for some
reason, is important to some people who do not want to be
known as divorced. It may also eliminate some troubling
alimony and community property problems. A judge can grant
alimony to a divorced person, but not to one who has never
been legally married. However, if you have children or if you
are the one with a property or alimony claim, you will not
want an annulment.

The length of the marriage is no bar to an annulment, by
the way. I once obtained an annulment for a man who had
been married for forty-six years. He had married young, then
left his wife after only a few weeks. He then came to Michigan,
found work, and remarried without having divorced his first
wife. Now he was ready for retirement and worried that his
second wife, to whom he had been married thirty-five years,
would be unable to collect on his social security and pension
accounts.

I filed a Complaint for Annulment or Divorce, something I
think I invented, and served it on the first wife, who we found
was still alive in Arkansas and had also remarried. The judge
granted the annulment on my client's testimony that he had
been forced into a "shotgun wedding" when he and the first
wife had been caught in a sexual situation by the girl's father.

Had our request for an annulment been denied, we would
then have asked for a divorce and my client would have had
to remarry his second wife to make it all legal.

## Are You Legally Married?

You might want to double-check your spouse's claim that she
is legally divorced from her first husband. If she is not, then
you are not legally married and can have your marriage
annulled. Also, be certain that your own marriage was legal.
Some people come to me assuming they have a "common
law" marriage. Once upon a time, people would be considered

legally married if they lived together openly as husband and wife for a set number of years. The courts recognized this type of marriage as perfectly legal. Nowadays, this type of informal marriage has been outlawed in most states. If you were married in a less than traditional ceremony, as was sometimes done in the free-spirited days of the seventies—that is, without a license, clergy, or judge—then you may not be married at all.

Check to see if you can get a copy of your marriage license from the state where you were married. If you cannot locate one, then maybe you are not married after all.

## Dangers of Divorce

There are several compelling reasons why a divorce can be the worst thing that ever happened to you. Divorce can be hazardous to your financial and even your physical health. If you are aging and/or have a poor medical history and are covered under your spouse's insurance, getting a divorce may mean that *you will never have medical or hospital insurance again*. Or, at the very least, you will pay a lot for it. Once divorced, your spouse has what the insurance companies call "no insurable interest" in you, and, therefore, you are on your own.

The same is true of life insurance. A divorce judgment eliminates the rights of the spouse as the beneficiary of any insurance policies on the other spouse. While you may be able to work a beneficiary designation into your separation agreement or divorce judgment, it is not something that is automatic. I have had several clients who came to me to try to help them collect the insurance benefits on their ex-husbands. The husbands never got around to changing the beneficiary, leaving the ex-wife on, just as she was when they were married, assuming that she would be able to collect on his death. The insurance companies rightly refused to pay to anyone other than the estate of the ex-husband, even though it was the intention of both of them that the ex-wife be the beneficiary. Unless he renamed her as such after the divorce, she cannot collect.

A divorced spouse also loses the "right of election" or "forced share." These are the rights in probate that a spouse has to the other's property in the event of death. Even if your spouse made a will leaving everything to his girlfriend, you, as the wife, can elect a statutory percentage of his estate no matter what the will says. (Assuming there is no premarital agreement, of course.) Once divorced, that right is gone. For example, assume that a wife has property in her sole name worth $100,000. She dies while still married, leaving a will that leaves everything to her two children and nothing to her husband. The husband has a right to choose either what the will leaves him—in this case nothing—or what the state law would leave him if there was no will. If there had been no will, in Michigan, for example, he would have been entitled to the first $60,000 and half the remainder for a total of $80,000. This right of election is gone if you are divorced because you are no longer an heir. Furthermore, once you are divorced you would also have no right to sue should your ex be killed as a result of someone else's negligence.

Be sure that you really want a divorce before you start proceedings. If it is your spouse who wants one and you do not, try to negotiate for a legal separation or a separation agreement.

## Timing: The Dangers of Divorcing Too Soon

Did you know that you can collect social security based upon the account of any spouse you have been married to for at least ten years? If you have been married nine years, it might be wise to wait a year to finalize that divorce. Whether you would be better off collecting on your own or your spouse's account depends upon your own earnings record, of course, but there are plenty of people out there who are counting on their spouse's social security when it comes to retirement. Although working in the home may be a productive and fulfilling occupation, you get no credit from social security for it unless you have been married for ten years to someone with an active account.

Timing can be critical. If your financial circumstances are about to change, you will want to time the divorce properly to take advantage of them. For instance, is your spouse about to receive a big bonus or a raise? Is she in line for a big promotion? Don't start divorce proceedings until the change is in effect. Waiting a little while can have a big payoff when it comes to working out a settlement.

However, if Aunt Millie has promised to leave her fortune to your spouse but there is nothing in writing, I would not delay the divorce thinking that you will get a share of the money—unless she is on her deathbed. People can live a lot longer than you might think.

As another example, let's say you are now in medical school and are sure the marriage is dead. Don't wait until you are licensed to get the divorce. Your medical degree can be a marital asset in most states. Divorcing sooner rather than later would in this case probably result in your paying less alimony or support than otherwise, and may prevent your medical degree from being considered a marital asset to be assigned a value and divided.

The judge looks at things as they stand right now, when he is listening to the evidence. Your speculation on what might or could happen in the future will have very little weight in his decision making. Who knows? You might never graduate from medical school. Your wife might not make partner after all. The judge only takes present circumstances into consideration when ruling on a settlement.

## Trickery, Lies, and Deceit

Leaving aside the moral issue of lying (it is not a nice thing to do), I have to say that it has helped many cases. Lying to your spouse is not illegal. In fact, there are probably very few couples heading toward divorce court who have always been totally honest with each other. Do not be surprised when your spouse lies to you. People do and say things when they are in a dissolving relationship that they might never have done or said before. Let's look at an example.

Helen came to my office at the behest of her sister, whose divorce I had handled a year or so earlier. She said she really did not want to fight the divorce her husband had filed but her sister did not trust the guy. Helen had come in to make her happy. She told me that her husband had told her the following things:

1. He had filed for an "uncontested divorce," which meant only one lawyer was needed. His lawyer would take care of all the paperwork and she did not need a lawyer at all. That way she did not have to go into court and it would all go through real smoothly.
2. Because he was the one who had worked and paid for the house while she stayed home, he could get the house if he wanted, but since he wanted to be fair, he would agree to sell it and give her what amounted to 20 percent of the equity.
3. He would give her custody and pay her 20 percent of his net pay as child support.
4. Since she was under age thirty, the judge would not give her alimony.

"Besides," Helen said, shifting nervously in her chair, "I don't have the money for a big court fight and he's giving me a pretty fair deal anyway." She just wanted me to look over the papers so she could tell her sister that she had seen a lawyer.

Everything Helen's husband had told her was a lie.

He was passing off completely bogus legal information, and she accepted it all as fact. To give him the benefit of the doubt, it is possible that he really believed what he was saying and intended only good things for her. But if she had relied on his advice, she would have really hurt herself.

### Legal Advice is for Lawyers

Do not take legal advice from your spouse. Aside from the fact that she may not know what she's talking about, she could be deliberately lying to you. You may be interested in knowing that when Helen's divorce was finalized, she got custody of the children, possession of the house until the youngest was eighteen, 35 percent of her husband's income as child support, payment by him of all their medical expenses, temporary alimony, and an equal division of all other marital property. The husband even paid my attorney fee. *And we did not even have a trial.* The case was settled between the lawyers based upon what we knew the judge would do if it went into court.

Both parties came out with a fair settlement and saved the expense and hassle of a messy trial.

This was not an unusual case. Many spouses lie to each other to gain advantage. It very often works.

Another tip: do not take legal advice from your friends and family. Everyone who has ever been through a divorce considers himself an expert on the subject and is perfectly willing to give you the benefit of his experience. Remember that each case is unique and what may have been true in your friend's/cousin's/colleague's case may not be true in yours. Get your legal advice from your lawyer.

### Lying to Courts and Others

If you are under oath, *do not lie*. It is perjury and a crime. Not that people don't do it. The fact is, it happens in nearly every trial. The judge's task—and it's not easy—is not only to determine who is deliberately lying, but to sort out what is a lie as opposed to simply a disparate point of view. Only the two spouses know if the judge has succeeded.

Do not lie to the judge. What you can and should do is tell your story from the point of view most favorable to you. You are under no obligation to tell more than you are asked. It is the attorney's responsibility to ferret out the information he wants from you. In a custody case I had, there was an allegation that my client's husband had allowed his girlfriend Donna to sleep over at the house while the children were there and his wife was at work. On questioning, he vehemently denied it, but volunteered that it was a completely different woman. The damage was done. He had given me information for which I might not have asked.

Who is to know what goes on in someone's mind? As we learned from many political scandals, from Richard Nixon to Bill Clinton, "I do not remember" is a convenient cop-out for those who are not about to admit wrongdoing.

Now, lying to court agencies is another matter. It is still wrong, and I don't recommend it, but in most cases it is not criminal if you are not under oath. In many court systems there is an agency called the "Friend of the Court" or "Division of Family Services" or some such name. This is the agency responsible for collecting and enforcing child support and visitation as well as for making recommendations to the judge on custody, support, and visitation after interviewing both parents. The interviews are confidential and sometimes anything goes. False allegations of neglect, drug and alcohol abuse, and physical abuse of the spouse and children are often made. A false allegation against you of sexual abuse of the children, even when proved to be untrue, can be disasterous to your divorce case. Just the allegation, even when it is shown to have been made falsely and maliciously, carries a stigma that cannot easily be shaken. If you believe your spouse is likely to lie about you, be sure not to pull any punches yourself. I have had more than one wife tell me that she did not report her husband's drug use because she did not want to make him look bad. Then she is surprised when the husband tells the agency a pack of lies about her mistreatment of the children and the worker recommends that he get custody.

Tell it like it is. A Friend of the Court report is given a lot of weight by a judge. Protect yourself. If your spouse has a bad history, tell it all, with specific examples. Give them names, dates, and places to back up your story. Do not hesitate to tell the truth about your spouse even if you have to reveal events in your marriage that you would prefer to keep private.

Of course, remember that you do not need to volunteer information about yourself that may be damaging. The worker knows nothing about you except what you tell her and what she hears from your spouse. Make her impression of you as favorable as possible by telling only the things about yourself that make you look good.

However, it is important that you tell everything that could be damaging to you to your attorney, even if you do not think the information will ever come out. If your spouse knows about it, you must be prepared for it to come up, and your attorney will not want to be surprised.

### Other Lies

I once had a woman call me in a panic. I had completed her divorce just a year before, giving her custody of her two chil-

dren and securing a court order barring her husband from seeing them except under supervision. Now he was gone with
the kids. It seems he had called her, asking to take the children, with his mother, to the ice-cream parlor just for an hour.
She'd agreed. She had found he had moved back to his country of origin, taking the children with him. Even though I had
taken the precaution of having the U.S. passports of the children canceled, he had new ones issued by his own government.
Our court order is not doing us much good right now. She
simply does not have the funds to fight him over there. She is
in serious trouble.

Because he lied and she believed him.

Note that the Geneva Convention, an international treaty
to which most Western nations subscribe, allows enforcement
of foreign custody orders. In 1986, the United States also rati-
fied the Hague Convention, which tries to curb international
child abductions by setting up judicial remedies to return
the child to the "country of habitual residence" where custody
would be decided.

If your spouse has taken the children from the country, it
is possible—if you have the time and money—to get help
from foreign courts.

If your spouse is in the U.S. military, the Adjutant
General's office will assist you in seeing that he complies with
the divorce judgment. Sometimes a letter to his commanding
officer will achieve results you cannot easily get in court.

The focus of this chapter has been to use some specific
examples to adequately warn you of your spouse's possible
lies. While I cannot ethically advise you to do so, you may
find that being the liar first will work just as effectively for
you as it would for your spouse.

# CHAPTER THREE

# GET CHILD CUSTODY: AVOID CHILD CASUALTIES

O nce upon a time there were no custody disputes in divorce cases. Children were considered "chattels," that is, property that belonged to the father, just like the cows, goats, and pigs. Fortunately, things changed. The pendulum swung in the other direction in the latter part of the nineteenth century with the "tender years presumption," which assumed that mothers were to be considered as a matter of law the best custodian of young children, that is, those of tender years. This presumption has continued until recently, and the younger the child, the stronger was the presumption that the mother was the best custodian. For a father to get custody he had to prove the mother "unfit," that is, that she was not morally or physically appropriate as a caretaker—a difficult thing to do most of the time.

Today, there are few legal presumptions about which parent is best suited for custody. Custody fights are very adversarial. Each parent tries to present the most evidence to support his or her claim. The modern trend in custody decision making is to base decisions on the "best interests of the child." There should no longer be a presumption in favor of one parent over the other just because of the sex of the parent or age of the child. To make decision making among courts and judges more uniform and predictable, many states have adopted a laundry list of factors to be evaluated in making a custody decision.

The list below is the one used in the state law of Michigan and a number of other states. Even if your state does not have such a list, you should use the factors I have listed in developing your custody plan. They are the most common factors looked at by judges everywhere, whether or not there is a specific list of factors in their statutes. In some cases these are much more than simple guidelines; some states require that a judge make specific findings of fact on each point and put them in writing. Give the judge reasons to find in your favor on each one and you greatly increase your chances of achieving your goals.

## Child Custody Factors

The sum total of these factors is used to determine what custody decision is in the best interests of the child.

- The love, affection, and other emotional ties existing between the parties involved and the child
- The capacity and disposition of the parties involved to give the child love, affection, guidance, and continuation of the education and raising of the child in his or her religion and creed, if any
- The capacity and disposition of the parties involved to provide the child with food, clothing, and medical care or other remedial care recognized and permitted under the laws of the state in place of medical care and other material needs
- The length of time the child has lived in a stable, satisfactory environment and the desirability of maintaining continuity
- The permanence as a family unit of the existing or proposed custodial home
- The moral fitness of the parties involved
- The mental and physical health of the parties involved
- The home, school, and community record of the child
- The reasonable preference of the child if the court finds the child to be of sufficient age and maturity to express preference
- The willingness and ability of each of the parents to facilitate and encourage a close and continuing relationship between the child and the other parent
- Any other factor considered by the court to be relevant to a particular child-custody dispute

Michigan has recently added another factor that must specifically be addressed by a judge making a custody decision. Evidence of domestic violence, or the lack of it, must be looked at by the judge even if the violence was not directed at or witnessed by the child.

## Your Custody Plan

A custody plan will help you and your attorney focus on both the strengths and the weaknesses of your custody case so that you can take appropriate measures to improve your position. Start your custody plan by using the chart in the next section. Notice that there are two columns—one for the father and one for the mother. Be honest with yourself and go down the chart giving yourself a point for each factor where you rate higher than your spouse, and her a point where she rates higher than you. You must be brutally realistic. While you probably believe yourself to be a very good parent, there is a difference between knowing what is true and being able to prove it. Factual evidence—that is, specific examples—is needed to support each area, or you do not get a point. Now add them up. Do you have more total points? If not, you know the areas in which you need to develop more evidence. This is not as simplistic an approach as it seems.

Evidence is the key here. Simply knowing in your own mind that you rate high in a certain area is not enough. You have to prove it. You need witnesses or documentary evidence for each factor. Your own testimony, while admissible, is just not good enough. I have been told by judges that the point system is exactly how they decide tough custody cases. So, gather evidence or examples to show your fitness on each and every factor listed.

I have seen many custody cases tried by attorneys who used only their own client's testimony to support their claim for custody. Unless the opposing lawyer does the same thing, they are not very successful. You need other witnesses. Bring in the school counselors, the teachers, and the principal. Have your clergyman testify for you. Bring in friends, family, and neighbors. Odds are you can muster quite a number of witnesses to testify on each of the factors.

So, what are you paying a lawyer for? People do expect the lawyer to gather the witnesses and prepare the case. And it is true that a good lawyer can sometimes overcome all your handicaps and still win for you. The fact is that lawyers take your case just as it is handed to them. Why take any chances? Even a mediocre lawyer can do a great job if you come to him with evidence and witnesses to support all the custody factors. Do not take chances on the most important decision someone else will make in your life.

Now let's look at some of the factors in more detail to give you an idea as to how to develop evidence and witnesses in each area. A witness (someone who can personally testify in court) is very good for your case. Any judge wants to be able to justify his or her decision on custody. If you provide not just your testimony, but also that of a half dozen other people who think you should get custody, then you have given the judge great justification for a decision in your favor.

*The love, affection, and other emotional ties existing between the parties involved and the children.*

An "expert" witness can carry the day here. An expert is a person who has particular expertise in the area being testified about because of her training, education, or experience. Have yourself and the children examined by a child psychologist (ask your lawyer or family doctor for a referral). Nothing is more convincing to a judge than the testimony of an expert that the children will suffer permanent psychological damage if they are removed from your custody.

Other potential witnesses are all around you. A baby-sitter, for instance, might say that the children asked for you at bedtime but not your spouse or that you were the one who made all the arrangements for their care and who called when away to see if they were okay. Other examples might be that you were always prompt in picking them up, while your spouse was chronically late or (more extreme, but it happens) your spouse appeared to have been drinking when he arrived to pick them up. In some cases, the children may have even seemed reluctant to go with him. Look for people who can give the judge specific examples like these, such as a daycare worker, teacher, or nurse—anyone who has seen the interaction between the competing parents and the child. Relatives do not make as good witnesses because they would be presumed to be biased toward you; but use them if they are all you have.

*The capacity and disposition of the parties involved to give the child love, affection, guidance and continuation of the education and raising of the child in his or her religion and creed, if any.*

Suppose you bring in the minister, priest, or rabbi who testifies that he often saw you and the children at services and that it was you who helped them with the summer picnic or the pancake breakfast. This creates a much more effective and lasting image in the mind of the judge than your bald statement that you love your children and will take them to church. If you have had a previous track record of successfully raising children from a prior marriage, certainly that fact should be brought out. Your testimony will, of course, be important to support this part of the custody plan since it refers to your ability and desire to provide love and care. Again, specific examples are helpful. What have you done in the past? Do you tuck them in and read bedtime stories every evening? If so, say it. I had a client who had people from the local village testify that they never saw the father come into town without his five-year-old son. Wherever the father went, he took the boy with him. They were a team.

*The capacity and disposition of the parties involved to provide the child with food, clothing, medical care, etc.*

"Disposition" is the important word here. Your financial ability to provide for the child's needs is not as important as your willingness and availability to do so. Having the money to buy the pony is not going to get you custody, but if you actually bought the pony it might help a little. The judge can always order the capable person to pay support. Whether it will be used for the benefit of the child is what is important. If a parent does not properly feed, clothe, or take care of the medical needs of a child, then he is not likely to be a good

choice for custody. Perhaps your spouse does not pay attention to the children's health as well as you do. Are you the one
who makes the dental appointments or decided that they
needed braces? Did you take them in for their immuniza-
tions? It may be that your spouse is too busy with her job to
take care of these things or it may be that the medical care of
the children is not a consideration for her.

The controversial case of little Miranda in Michigan is a
good example. A judge took custody away from the mother
because she was going back to school and would be placing
the child in daycare. The father showed that he lived with his
parents and that his mother would be available to take care of
the child. That fact alone was what swayed the judge in favor
of the father.

However, this factor is most often used against the parent
who has a support arrearage. The reasoning is that if a parent
had the disposition to take care of his children, he would not
owe money for their support. It is nearly impossible to get a
successful custody case going if the parent wanting custody
owes support. I insist that my clients either pay up their back
child support or have a definite repayment agreement set up
in writing before we start a custody case. If you want to get
custody of the children, you had better not be behind in child
support payments.

*The length of time the child has lived in a stable, satisfactory
environment and the desirability of maintaining continuity.*

This can be one of the strongest arguments you have for
maintaining custody if you already have it. A whole body of
law has developed around determining what is an "established
custodial environment" (ECE).

What the courts are trying to do is minimize the disrup-
tion of the child's life. The divorce is thought to be traumatic
enough for the kids without them also having to leave their
home, friends, neighborhood, and school. If a strong parent-
child relationship has formed, courts are loath to break it.
Some states have gone so far as to define an established custodial environment by statute. Michigan's Child Custody Act is
an example of common language:

"An established custodial environment is created if, over an appreciable period of time, the child naturally looks to the custodian in such an environment for guidance, discipline, the necessities of life, and parental comfort."

The time element varies. For very young children an ECE can be created in only a few months since they bond much more quickly. For a teenager it can take much longer.

What this means is that judges do not like to tinker with custody if the current situation seems to be working. If a child is settled, safely and happily, why uproot him? Thus, it is very important, if you want custody, to stay with the children no matter what. You do not want your spouse establishing the custodial environment.

In the initial custody decision, the court is governed by what is called a "preponderance of evidence." This means that the court will favor the party who shows, by even the slightest margin, that he or she is the best person to care for the children. It is as if you and your spouse are balanced on either side of a seesaw; the one who tips the scale even the least bit will be the winner.

However, once an ECE has been set up by one of the parents, the amount of evidence necessary to change that environment becomes much greater. To make a change you would have to show by "clear and convincing evidence" that it is in the best interests of the child to change custody. Clear and convincing evidence is a lot more evidence than the preponderance of the evidence. Using the seesaw analogy, the winning side would be sitting on the ground while the loser would be trapped high in the air.

The message should be obvious here: keep the children with you at all costs. Try to be the one who has the children so that you are the one who gets the temporary custody order. When a divorce case starts, it is most often the case that one parent moves out of the home, leaving the children with the other. The one in the home usually has temporary legal custody and primary possession. If it takes a year or more to bring the custody case to trial, the one in the home with the children has an ECE just by virtue of the temporary order. In this kind of situation the judge is not basing his decision on a preponderance of evidence but on clear and convincing evidence. Once that ECE is shown to exist, you have created a much more difficult case for your opposition.

If you cannot have the children with you, or your spouse already has the children and has had them for some time, the best thing for you to do is spend as much time with them as you can. Try to organize your living arrangements so that your children have their own bedroom(s) at your home as well as their own set of possessions and clothing. Make the place a real home for them since that is what you are working toward.

*The permanence as a family unit of the existing or proposed custodial home.*

Show the judge your plans for a stable family relationship should you be awarded custody. By outlining your proposed living situation and comparing it with that of the other parent you may be able to sway the judge to your side.

This factor can particularly come into play if you are proposing to change custody after the divorce is over. If you have remarried, and live in your children's current school district, a judge may deem yours a more stable family situation than that of your former spouse.

Another situation might be where your spouse wants one of the children but not all of them. Courts are reluctant to separate siblings unless there is a very good reason for doing so. If you have a plan to keep them together, your plan is more likely to be favored. I had a client, for example, who had another child by a previous marriage who was only two years older than her child by the present spouse. The court awarded her custody of the younger child primarily because of the close relationship between the two children.

Keep in mind that behind all these factors is the "best interests of the child," not the best interests of the parents.

*The moral fitness of the parties involved.*

While many states will not allow "fault" to be considered in making the decision to grant the divorce, some do allow fault to be used to determine custody if it reflects upon the character of the proposed custodian. The traditional fault ground, and the one used most often in granting divorces, was adultery. In custody cases, we are looking at the comparative "moral fitness" of the parents.

Moral fitness can be more than just one party committing adultery. You would surely want the court to know if your spouse was an alcoholic or had a violent temper. Similarly, it is relevent to let the court know that your spouse or his friends are habitual users of drugs. While you may not have any circumstances quite as extreme as these, you must play up your own good moral character and expose the bad things about your spouse. But do not run a "smear campaign" that might irritate the judge. He may just decide that both of you are unfit for custody.

Be alert to how the moral fitness factor can work against you too. Judges can be hypocritical and falsely righteous just like anyone else. I have seen a judge whose own character was rather questionable threaten to remove custody from a parent because her boyfriend lived in the house with her and the children, even though their wedding was set for a few months later. They got married immediately and the judge was satisfied. So, the rule is to be discreet if you cannot be completely above reproach.

*The mental and physical health of the parties involved.*
While it should be clear that the court will not award custody to a known insane or comatose person, the lesser degrees of physical and mental incapacity can cause problems.

Here is a strategy that few attorneys use even though it is available in the court rules of most states: If the mental or physical ability of a litigant is relevant to the matter at issue, a court can order a person to undergo a physical or mental examination and have the results reported to the judge. If you seriously believe that your spouse has a recognizable emotional disorder or a physical problem that would affect his ability to take care of your child, you should see about petitioning the court for an examination. But watch out if you have a history of instability or physical problems yourself. Attorneys are great at retribution and you may find yourself being examined as well.

This factor may be very relevant if the person seeking custody is a grandparent. The court would be concerned that the proposed custodian be physically able to take care of the needs of the children as well as likely to live to see them raised to maturity.

### The home, school, and community record of the child.

For older children, in particular, this factor is very important. The children's performance in school while living with you as their primary caretaker is looked at closely by the judge. If they are doing well, you will want to bring in teachers, coaches, and activity directors to testify for you.

On the home side, the judge will want to know if you have discipline problems with them or if the children have been in trouble in the community. Again, emphasize your good record with them and the poor performance of your spouse in guiding the behavior of the children. How the kids do in school and in the neighborhood is something that the court will either hold against you or give you credit for.

### The reasonable preference of the child if the child is deemed to be of sufficient age and maturity to express preference.

The older the child is, the more weight will be given his or her preference. There are even jurisdictions such as Florida in which the child can get a lawyer herself and petition for a change of custody without either parent's consent.

How the judge finds out a child's preference is important. We all want to keep the children off the witness stand, where they are subject to cross-examination. The judge will usually talk to children "in camera," that is, in private, out of the courtroom. The judge can then put the children at ease and talk informally with them to find out their preference. Lawyers and parents may not even be allowed to be present during this interview.

We know that the average child would prefer to live with both parents and that it is placing a difficult burden on his shoulders to ask him to pick the parent he prefers. He may feel that by making a choice he is double-crossing the other parent. That is why we try everything possible to prepare the case well so that it can be settled without actually going to trial. Be sure that if the judge hears a preference from the child that it is his or her true choice.

Parents will try to influence children to make choices that may not be in their best interests. I remember one case in which a ten-year-old boy told the judge he wanted to live with his father. A week later, when we were back in court, he said he wanted to talk to the judge again. This time he said he wanted to live with his mother. When the judge asked him why he had changed his mind he said, "Well, my dad said that if I lived with him, he would take me to Walt Disney World, then he didn't do it so I want to be with my mom."

Judges do listen to the child's preference, but the weight they give that preference depends upon the child's age and maturity. Judges know that parents try to influence the decisions of their children. Remember that the first question a judge might ask is, "What did your parents tell you to say to me?" It will not look good for you if your child reveals that you gave him a script to repeat that did not reflect the child's true wishes.

Judges also know that sometimes a child will prefer living with a parent who will administer the least discipline or be more lax in enforcing rules of behavior. If your spouse is the type who allows the children free reign—e.g., shows little concern for them doing their homework, bathing regularly, or keeping regular hours—you will want to be sure to show that in court to offset any damage the child's preference for that parent may have caused your case. Children do not always know what is in their best interests.

*The willingness and ability of each of the parents to facilitate and encourage a close and continuing relationship between the child and the other parent.*

The custody laws recognize the importance to children of a continuing relationship with both parents after the divorce. After all, the parents are getting divorced, not the kids. You will be judged on your efforts to keep your children involved with your spouse. Do not be openly hostile to the other parent or put him down in front of the children. For one thing, the children will naturally be very defensive and protective of the other parent and may resent you for your attitude. For another thing, you can be sure that anything you say will get back to the other side. The worst thing you can do, if you have custody, is deny your spouse visitation. It is very tempting to use visitation as reward or punishment for paying or not paying support. Resist the temptation. Do not use your children this way. It is not fair to them and judges do not like it.

Do not go too far, however, in trying to encourage the relationship with the other parent. I have heard of cases where the custodial parent has actually sued the other to try and force visitation. These suits cannot be successful. While you can force someone to pay support, you cannot force them into visitation. Even if you put the parent and the child into the same room, you are not establishing a healthy parent-child relationship if the parent is there involuntarily. Having a relationship with your children is a voluntary choice.

*Any other factor considered by the court to be relevant to a particular child custody dispute.*

This is a catchall provision. Just because something relevant to the custody decision does not fit into one of the categories above is no reason to ignore it. If you feel something is relevant to the custody case, be sure to include it in your plan. The existence of domestic violence against either you or your children would certainly be relevant.

## Custody Plan Checklist

Use this chart to rate yourself and your spouse in the areas listed. Give yourself one point for each of the factors where you "win" and give your spouse points for the areas that he or she wins. Factor number four is worth two points and factor number nine earns two points if the average age of the children is over ten years and three points if they are over fourteen.

| Factor | Father | Mother |
|---|---|---|
| 1. Love, affection, and emotional ties | | |
| 2. The capacity and disposition of the parties involved to give the child love, affection, and guidance | | |
| 3. The capacity and disposition of the parties involved to provide the child with food, clothing, and medical care | | |
| 4. The length of time the child has lived in a stable, satisfactory environment | | |
| 5. The permanence as a family unit of the existing or proposed custodial home | | |
| 6. Moral fitness | | |
| 7. Mental and physical health | | |
| 8. The home, school, and community record | | |
| 9. The preference of the child | | |
| 10. The willingness and ability to encourage a relationship with the other parent | | |
| 11. Any other relevant factor(s) | | |
| Total points for each side: | | |

## Joint Custody

The trend today is away from awarding sole custody and toward giving it to both parents. The primary consideration in approving joint custody is the ability of the parents to cooperate in making important decisions affecting the child. Consequently, it is rare for a judge to award joint custody after a contested custody battle, though it does happen. The parents have already proved that they are unable to agree or they would not be in court asking the judge to make the decision for them.

Joint custody, therefore, is almost always a result of a divorce settlement, though in a few states, such as Michigan, the judge must tell the parents about the availability of joint custody.

In some states, the judge must, by law, award joint custody if the parties have agreed to it—unless there is clear and convincing evidence that such an arrangement is not in the best interests of the child. (Now you know what all those legal words mean.) The reason for passing such a law is that some judges do not like joint custody and were refusing to award it even when the parties had agreed to it.

One of the primary criticisms of joint custody I have heard from Friend of the Court workers and some of my colleagues has been that the arrangement simply gives the parents another topic of contention and its effect is to merely postpone the custody fight. I find that argument without merit and have seen hundreds of joint custody agreements that work fine.

The physical arrangements of the agreement can be as varied as the imagination and circumstances permit. Some are no different than typical sole custody–visitation arrangements, while others can be quite elaborate. In some cases children actually alternate their time between parents, living at one house one week and another the following week. Of course, the parents should live in the same school district for this arrangement to work. Children sometimes object to the constant upheaval in their lives inherent in such a ping-pong living style.

It is more common to have agreements where the child lives with one parent during the school year and the other during summer vacation. In one unusual situation, the children remained in the former marital home and the parents took turns moving in and out. They even shared the cost of an apartment to live in when it was not their turn with the children. In all joint custody arrangements, you must be allowed visitation when the children are with your ex-spouse.

Like all custody awards, joint custody is not necessarily permanent. The court has the power to change any custody order at any time based on what is in the best interests of the children.

The lesson here is to not forget your custody plan even after the divorce is over and you have won custody. Changed circumstances can land you right back in court.

## Child Support Arrearages

We have all heard of "deadbeat dads." The nonsupport payers who have to be hounded and chased down to force them to support their children. These dads are depicted as living in luxury while their children are living on public assistance. In fact, that situation has existed in the past and is still the case occasionally. Child support awards have traditionally been difficult to enforce, but changes in the law have made enforcement easier. Federal and state laws not only allow support to be deducted directly from the paycheck of the person ordered to pay it, but in some cases require it. In addition, laws now allow arrearages in support to be taken from any state or federal tax refunds that a payer may be entitled to receive. If you are the one receiving support and there is an existing arrearage, get in contact with the court agency in your state responsible for collection. They can help you collect your back support free of charge. You can assist them by advising them of your former spouse's employment and current address.

If you are unable to get help from the government agencies, you may hire an attorney and petition for collection yourself. The contempt-of-court power can be of great help in enforcing payment.

If you are a support payer and owe an arrearage, you may be able to get the arrearage lowered. Unless your spouse has been on public assistance, you are allowed to make a deal directly with her to reduce the amount owed. Perhaps you have provided noncash goods or services that can offset the amount owed. If the two of you agree, the courts will automatically reduce the amount on the books. A spouse owed a large arrearage may even consider an agreement to take a lump-sum payment of less than the amount due in order to clear the whole matter up.

Arrearages owed to the state because your spouse once received public assistance for the children can also be reduced by agreement with the prosecutor in charge of collecting those arrearages. Prosecutors have the authority in most cases to settle the amount owed, so you may be able to offer a lump-sum payment of less than the amount on the books to clear the entire arrearage. A lawyer can assist you in making such an arrangement. Remember that if your spouse was receiving Aid to Dependent Children payments, only the state can make a settlement agreement. Your spouse has no authority to make a deal since the arrearage belongs to the state, not the spouse.

If you are a support payer, be sure to make payment either directly through the court system or, if you pay your spouse directly, by check. It is very important to be able to prove that you made the payments you say you made. Cash payments should not be made unless you receive a written receipt in return.

If you are a support receiver, or are likely to be, you should be sure to have some provision put in your divorce judgment to assure continued payments even in the case of the death of your spouse. I recommend that children be made irrevocable beneficiaries of the support payer's life insurance or that he post some kind of security to assure payment. This can be part of your total settlement package.

# CHAPTER FOUR

# BEFORE YOU CALL IN THE
# TROOPS: SELF-HELP

The ideal divorce plan starts before any proceedings are commenced in court. Once court proceedings are initiated, strict legal rules must be followed and the court has control of your property, your children, and in some ways, your future. It is important, therefore, to take all the protective actions you can before the divorce starts. In other words, help yourself. "Self-help" in a legal sense means taking care of matters yourself without going through the legal system. Rather than jump right into a divorce proceeding where your spouse has the benefit of hired help (see chapter 8), it is sometimes wise to take matters into your own hands first—without a lawyer and before the divorce proceedings start. The two primary reasons to use self-help are to get what the courts will not give you and to weaken your opponent's case.

## Helping Yourself to What You Want

In the first place, it is highly unlikely that the legal system will give you what you really want. For example, you really want all the money in the joint bank account so that you can buy a boat and sail to Tahiti. As one human being to another, I might say that that isn't a fair thing to do to your spouse. But purely from a legal standpoint, all I can say is go ahead and take it. Joint money belongs as much to you as to your spouse. Once you have the boat and are sailing away, there isn't much anyone can do about it. At least not until you get back. Then you may find that the assets you squandered are to be deducted from your share of the total marital property division.

The point is that unless there is a court order or a law forbidding something, you are free to do it. Be sure though that you discuss your proposed action and its possible ramifications with your attorney first. Not that you have to hire a lawyer right then to do a divorce, but use one on an advisory basis to discuss and plan possible courses of action to be certain that your plan is legal. What is legally permissible and what is morally right are not always the same. Fairness is a concept for the courts to apply. Do not expect your spouse to be as fair to you as you would be to him. Unfortunately, the golden rule does not seem to apply in marital dissolutions, as you will see from the following examples.

Tina was a twenty-two-year-old woman who had been married only a little more than a year. There were no children and both parties worked full-time. She came to me in tears after she had come home from work one day and found their apartment completely empty. Every piece of furniture and all the dishes were gone. Her clothes were in a pile in the closet; even the hangers had been taken. The food in the cupboards and refrigerator was missing. The carpeting had been removed from the floors. There was no note or explanation. Thinking at first that she had been robbed, she called the police from a pay phone (the telephone was missing too), then phoned her mother-in-law looking for Rob, her husband.

The mother-in-law said he was not there and did not want to see her anymore. She refused to discuss the removal of the apartment's contents or reveal where Rob had gone. Tina said there had never been any trouble between them and she was totally surprised by this turn of events.

We found out later that Rob had accepted a job transfer and moved to another city. He had apparently planned his departure some time in advance. We filed for divorce and got a court order for the return of some of the personal property, but it was clear that the costs involved in enforcing the order would exceed the value of the property that could be recovered. Rob ended up not only with most of the marital property, but also a divorce paid for by his wife. Tina was victimized by her jerk husband who effectively used self-help to get what he wanted.

Another example: Jody and Sam had three children, all under the age of ten. Sam worked in an automobile factory and Jody had a part-time job as a cashier at a local discount store. Sam was from the area and had a large extended family all living nearby. Jody had moved from Kentucky and her family was still there. Sam controlled the money in the household, even requiring Jody to turn over her paycheck to him each week. He gave her an allowance for food and things for the children, but she had to provide receipts to show what she spent.

Jody was afraid of her husband and entirely economically dependent upon him. When she finally came to see me for advice, after breaking two previous appointments, she was desperately unhappy and wanted out of the marriage. She wanted me to make the final decision for her, to tell her to file for divorce. An attorney cannot do that. All I could do was explain the various options open to her and the ramifications of each option. She then had to decide what to do.

After I had explained divorce, alimony, support, custody, property division, counseling, and other divorce alternatives, Jody asked, "What if I just leave? You know, take the kids to my mom's." She said she was afraid that he and his family would make life hell for her if she stayed. She needed the emotional support of her family in Kentucky.

There were no custody orders in effect at the time. The kidnapping laws (see the Parental Kidnapping Prevention Act reproduced in appendix F) therefore did not apply. I explained that she could file for divorce in another jurisdiction once she established proper residency provided that he did not file first here. I did not see her again but she wrote several months later to tell me that she had gone ahead and taken the children, the credit cards, and as much stuff as would fit into their van and moved to Kentucky. She had seen a lawyer there who told her he could get child support, temporary custody, and possibly even alimony for her.

Had Jody stayed in Michigan we could probably have gotten custody, alimony, child support, and a fair division of the

marital property, but she would not have been able to take
the children from this jurisdiction without the permission of the
court. She also would have had to fight the battle on her own
without the moral support of her family. Jody got what she
really wanted by taking action on her own, after consulting a
lawyer, and without jumping into a divorce case with her eyes
closed.

Remember that in Jody's case there was no custody order in
effect and no divorce case had been started. If there is a custody order, even a temporary one, and you remove the children
from the jurisdiction of the court that entered the order, you
can be charged with kidnapping and wind up in jail. If there is
no court order, then each parent has equal rights to custody
and control of the children and can take them anywhere.

The point of the above examples is that if there is no court
order or law forbidding it, anything goes. People sometimes
do take the children, take the money, charge the credit cards
to the limit, and disappear quite legally.

## Weakening Your Opponent

As I mentioned earlier, the second way to use self-help is to
weaken your opponent's case. If you are planning on doing
battle in divorce court, it is far wiser to enter the ring against
an adversary who has few weapons with which to fight you. It
is up to you to disarm your spouse.

First you must analyze all the possible areas of contention.
What does your spouse want—and what do you have to lose?

For example, if custody is what will be the issue, then proper
preparation and recordkeeping is necessary as explained in
chapter 1. If you have kept a detailed record over a long period of time of the specific things you did to support each of
the "best interests of the children" criteria, and your spouse
has nothing but her memory to rely on, you will have the
upper hand. By the time the divorce is filed, you will have
prepared your case by having done specific documented
things that the judge can see and verify to add weight to your
case. Your spouse is weakened because she has not preserved
and prepared her custody case.

Following are other areas in which you can help to change the odds:

### Child Support

You can minimize or maximize the amount of child support paid by manipulating the circumstances. Although formulas vary from state to state and even county to county within the same state, child support is generally based upon a percentage of the noncustodial parent's net income and in thirty-one states includes a reduction based upon the earnings of the custodial parent. Seventeen states use the straight percent of income rule with no reduction for the custodial parent's income. The rest use an allocation process called the "Melson formula," which tries to balance support between the parents after determining a base minimum level of support for the children and having that shared by the parents.

Therefore, if you are likely to be the support payer, it is wise, if possible, to keep your income down and your spouse's income up for the year or so preceding the divorce filing. You might think about having additional taxes withheld from your check to decrease your net earnings. You will get it back later in the form of a tax refund. This strategy may be caught by the court or your spouse's attorney, but then again maybe it won't. There is nothing illegal about it and it often works.

Encouraging your spouse to work and even assisting him or her will only benefit you if you are the payer. Assistance can be in the form of helping him find work or possibly getting him work in the family business or you watching the children or arranging daycare to allow your spouse the time for a job search.

Self-help is important in planning for the future because what you do now to set a support level will be in effect for a long time, and even a small additional amount each week adds up over the years. Remember that while support levels can be changed after the divorce, some courts have restrictions, for instance, allowing changes only every two years except in unusual circumstances. Therefore, you should fight very hard from the outset to get the most or pay the least. And keep in mind that unless a custodial spouse is receiving public assistance, many states will allow any level of support (even no support at all) so long as both parents agree. Remember this when you are trying to get your separation agreement signed. Just because there is a recommended support schedule in your state does not necessarily mean that you and your spouse cannot agree on a different amount—whether higher or lower. Even where the state law says that the state support schedule must be used, there are ways to get a different agreed-upon amount if the correct procedure is followed. Check your local law to see if you and your spouse can set your own support amount.

### Property Division

One of the major problems in dividing property involves the marital home, particularly if there are minor children. The house is, for most couples, the major asset of the marriage. They both have an interest in it and usually both count on at least part of the equity if not the house itself to sustain them after the divorce is final. Judges like to give possession of the house to the custodial parent until the children are of legal age. The noncustodial spouse will usually get a lien against the property payable on the sale of the property or upon the youngest child reaching the age of majority, whichever comes first.

If you are the likely custodial parent, or want to be, do not move out of the house. It is very difficult to argue that you need the house for the children if you and they have already left it and are living elsewhere. True, it is often difficult to live in the same house with a spouse whom you are divorcing, but consider whether it might be worth it if it means getting what you really want.

There is a flip side of this issue, of course, for the likely noncustodial parent. Before any divorce action starts, try to get rid of the house or get your spouse out of it. You could offer to rent her an apartment for a trial separation. Or sell the house and move the whole family into an apartment while you "look for just the right kind of place to move into."

You might also consider getting a second mortgage on your home. This accomplishes two things. First, it removes much of the equity, which can then be divided or used to pay you for your interest in it. Second, you have made the place more expensive to live in by now having two mortgage payments on it so that it may not be practical for your spouse to stay there.

### Removing and Concealing Property

Although often done, removing and concealing property can be *undone* if the spouse's attorney finds out about it. If you are tempted to hide or conceal assets, keep the following story in mind:

I had a client whose husband gradually converted much of his company's profits into gold coins that he bought with cash from an out-of-state dealer. He then declared bankruptcy and filed for divorce. He thought he was being pretty slick, but the bankruptcy trustee was able to trace the cash to the coins and got much of it back. He was prosecuted for fraud and much of the money was eaten up by court costs and creditors. His wife only got some of what she was entitled to, but had the satisfaction of seeing him in jail.

Self-help can also be used to weaken your opponent's will to fight. Carl, a thirty-three-year-old husband and father of two, had just left his wife, Jan, and filed for divorce. Initially hurt and shocked, Jan's emotions quickly turned to anger. When Carl embarked on a new relationship, she was even more incensed. She focused her energies on fighting him for everything, refusing to negotiate the smallest point.

Whether he did it as an act of kindness or whether it was a devious trick I cannot say, but Carl finally managed to distract Jan from the divorce proceedings. He convinced one of her close friends, who was single, to take her to a Parents Without Partners meeting. Jan loved it. She found men who were willing to dance with her, something Carl would never do, and developed an independent social life. The divorce went more smoothly from then on and was settled without trial. Something similar may or may not work for you, but might be worth a try.

# CHAPTER FIVE

# CEASE-FIRE: THE ENFORCEABLE SEPARATION AGREEMENT

This is potentially the most important chapter of this book. It describes a tool that can save countless hours of misery, lots of money, and get a great end result for yourself. It can eliminate the stress of litigation and make the whole divorce go through much more quickly. In fact, it will render your spouse unable to contest the case in many states.

The tool is the separation agreement. Before you file for divorce and while you are still able to talk about such things with your spouse, try to negotiate one. This is a contract, in writing, spelling out the complete terms of custody, support, property division, and alimony after you separate and during your separation. And it contains a provision that these terms will be followed in the event a divorce is started later on. In most states, a properly drawn separation agreement can be included as part of the divorce judgment and is then enforceable by the court to the same extent as if the judge himself had made the decision. Of course, you cannot make an agreement that usurps the power of the court in matters of custody, support, and alimony; the court has the power to make its own decision in these areas, if called for, but the areas involving the property division are enforceable as agreed. If the agreement has been entered into voluntarily with full disclosure of all assets by both sides and both sides having the opportunity to obtain independent counsel before signing it, the parts concerning property cannot then be changed if your spouse decides, upon filing for divorce, that she does not like the deal she has made. If you do not ever divorce, the agreement is enforceable in civil court as a contract, but if you do divorce, the terms of the separation agreement will likely be the terms of the later divorce judgment.

A separation agreement is entered into after the marriage starts and is not the same as a prenuptial agreement, which is signed before the couple marries. The law treats these agreements differently, with the separation agreement being more universally enforceable than the prenuptial agreement. The rationale of the courts is that public policy favors settlement over litigation.

It is far easier to get a separation agreement signed than it is to settle a divorce where both sides have lawyers representing them in an ongoing adversarial court case. One reason is that at this early stage, one spouse is often hoping that the other will "come to his senses" and resume the marriage. That spouse will thus not be too hard-nosed in negotiating an agreement that she views as merely temporary. In fact, both parties might really be hoping that the agreement will not have to lead to a divorce. Another reason is that most of the negotiating will be done strictly between the two spouses, with no lawyers involved until the agreement is reached. In the early stages of the separation, typically, the mutual animosity has not escalated to the point where the parties are not talking at all. The time to discuss the separation agreement is when the separation itself is being discussed.

It is to the benefit of both parties to have the terms of the separation in writing to avoid misunderstanding as to the rights and obligations of each person. Discussing settlement after one or both sides have retained lawyers becomes more difficult, since at that point all decisions must be cleared by the attorneys. Furthermore, as an unresolved divorce case "ages," the rising anger and emotion make settlement more difficult.

If your spouse is suggesting a divorce, it makes sense for you to suggest a separation agreement first, on a trial basis, before taking the drastic divorce step. You can justify the creation of a separation agreement by saying that it is to protect both of your interests during the trial separation. You are really looking out for him! You do not have to say the word "divorce" at this point. I have included a sample separation agreement at the end of this chapter. Use it as a general outline, but be sure to have your final agreement approved by your lawyer.

After you have worked out all the details of your separation agreement with your spouse, your lawyer will make sure it is in the proper form and will be enforced if a divorce is filed later. It should contain a provision that both spouses have had the benefit of independent counsel and that full disclosure of all assets has been made by both parties.

Although not a strict requirement in all states, I recommend that you tell your spouse to take it to a lawyer to have it reviewed. This independent review lessens the chance that the court will say the agreement was involuntarily signed or is unfair. A lawyer reviewing a settlement agreement brought in by a client will not be in the same advocacy position as one representing a client in a divorce case. He is merely being hired to approve in legal form an accomplished settlement, not fight the other spouse.

Your spouse's lawyer for this purpose cannot be the same one you use. He needs his own separate, independent counsel. You can suggest a lawyer for him if you like, but you would be wise not to recommend an experienced divorce specialist who might want to rewrite the whole thing to favor your spouse. Talk to your spouse about the importance of keeping the role of the lawyer to a minimum and suggest that, to save money, the job of your spouse's attorney be limited to approving the wording of the agreement.

Stress the "trial separation" aspect of the agreement, but do not use that phrase in the document. Your intent is that this document be enforceable if the trial separation becomes a permanent one. The reason you need to emphasize to your spouse the "trial" part is to make him less reluctant to sign. Remember your goal: get what you really want with as little trouble and cost as possible. The important thing is not what your spouse thinks is the effect of the agreement—whether it is a "trial" agreement or not—but that you get what you really want in the separation agreement and get it signed and approved.

The "full disclosure" part of the agreement means that if you have hidden assets and your spouse discovers them later, the agreement is off as to those assets. You cannot engage in what the court would call fraudulent behavior. The agreement must be entered into by both parties having their legal eyes wide open, even if they have hopes that the separation agreement will not result in a divorce.

Remember though that the court retains jurisdiction over child custody and support levels, so that portion of the agreement may be subject to change.

Trying for the separation agreement is a worthwhile investment of your time. It may shave months from the divorce process, result in a quick and favorable settlement, and save a lot of money and stress for both of you. Remember that you can argue that the agreement protects your spouse's rights as well as your own. If you cannot get your spouse to sign, you have lost very little and have at least introduced him to the concept of bargaining over the issues.

All the important issues should be decided in the separation agreement. The section for division of property should dispose of all the property each of you has separately or in joint names. Decide who gets the house and how the other spouse is to be paid for his interest in it. Or is the house to be sold and the proceeds of the sale divided? If it is, what will the split be? Who will live there until it is sold? Who pays the mortgage, taxes, insurance, and maintenance until the sale of the home?

For other property, you should specifically list each item and who gets it, including furniture and household items. Debts are also in the following agreement. Be sure to remove your spouse's name from any joint credit and joint checking accounts. Divide the credit card accounts up and notify the credit card companies that only one person now has authority to charge.

The following sample agreement can serve as an outline for you, but refer to the specific areas of this book on support, custody, alimony, and property before agreeing to anything. Be absolutely certain that the agreement gives you everything that you really want and, if possible, a little more to use for bargaining later on in the event of a contested divorce proceeding.

This document is intended as a general outline only. After filling out your own separation agreement in this format, take it to the lawyer you have selected to put it into a form enforceable in your state. When you hire a lawyer to approve it, you are relying on his or her professional expertise. If this type of agreement is enforceable in your state, your lawyer legally assumes any liability if it proves to be unenforceable and will therefore be very careful to put it into the best possible form.

## SAMPLE SEPARATION AGREEMENT

THE PARTIES, _____
(hereinafter called the "Wife" in this document) and
_____ (hereinafter called
the "Husband" in this document) have made this
agreement to settle the rights each may have in the
issues of their marriage since they have now decided
to live apart. The terms of this agreement shall govern
their legal rights during the time of their separation
and shall be enforceable as a contract between them
since they are each giving up and gaining valuable
consideration. The terms of this agreement shall be
included in any later divorce or separate maintenance
action filed between the parties to the full extent
allowed by the law of the state in which such a legal
action might be filed. The property that each party
receives in the property division section shall be the
entire property to which each party is entitled even in
the event of the death of either party and each party
gives up his or her right to dower, family allowance,
or any statutory forced share of the estate of the other.

*SECTION I: Custody of Minor Children*
The names and dates of birth of all children born to
the parties or adopted by them during the marriage
are as follows:

Name                                    Date of Birth

It is agreed that the Wife shall have the sole custody of
the following minor children:

It is agreed that the Husband shall have the sole custody of the following minor children:

It is agreed that both parents shall have joint custody
of the following minor children:

The parties understand that any custody agreement is
subject to the approval of the appropriate court to decide
custody in the event of a divorce or legal separation.

DEFINITION: "Custody" means the decision-making
authority and responsibility for important decisions
regarding the child. Joint Custody means both parents
share in that authority and responsibility.

REMOVAL OF CHILD(REN) FROM STATE: It is
agreed that neither parent shall remove a child's residence from the state of residence as existed on the
date of this agreement without the notarized written
permission of the other parent.

*SECTION II: Visitation*
It is agreed that the noncustodial parent shall have reasonable visitation with the minor child(ren) in the custody of the other parent as they shall agree, or

It is agreed that visitation with the minor child(ren) shall be given according to the following schedule in addition to any other times to which the parents may agree:

*SECTION III: Healthcare Expenses*
It is agreed that the Husband shall be responsible for the healthcare expenses and for providing hospitalization and medical insurance on the following children:

It is agreed that the Wife shall be responsible for the healthcare expenses and for providing hospitalization and medical insurance on the following children:

If a noncustodial parent is providing health care insurance for the children, he or she shall turn over to the custodial parent such identification cards or forms as shall be necessary to procure services under the terms of such policy of insurance.

DEFINITION: "Healthcare expenses" means those reasonable and necessary healthcare expenses normally incurred when providing for a known or provable need.

*SECTION IV: Support Payments*
CHILD SUPPORT: The Husband shall pay the following amount of weekly child support (in cash, not ser-

vices or goods) to the Wife for each of the following children until each 1) reaches eighteen years of age, or 2) graduates from high school, or 3) until (insert here "graduates from college," if that is your agreement).

Child's Name                              Amount of Weekly Support

The Wife shall pay the following amount of weekly child support (in cash, not services or goods) to the Husband for each of the following children until each 1) reaches eighteen years of age, or 2) graduates from high school, or 3) until (insert here "graduates from college," if that is your agreement).

SPOUSAL SUPPORT: The Husband/Wife (strike out one) shall pay to the Husband/Wife the amount of $_____ per _____ until _____ (Insert a specific date, or a specific contingency such as remarriage or completion of schooling).

ARREARAGES IN SUPPORT: It is agreed that any arrearages in child or spousal support shall be preserved and collectible in any later divorce or separate maintenance action.

SECTION V: Property Division
The parties have both fully disclosed all their assets to each other. A list of the joint assets and each party's separate assets are attached to this agreement as appendix I. Each party has also fully disclosed his or her income to the other party.

The property shall be divided as follows: (insert here the specific division of all property of the marriage including real estate, vehicles, accounts, stocks, and personal property). The property division is attached to this agreement as appendix II.

DEBTS: The debts of the parties are to be paid as follows:

Name of Creditor     Amount Owed     To Be Paid By

FURTHER AGREEMENTS:

Both parties enter into this agreement without duress and with full knowledge of the extent of the other party's assets. BOTH PARTIES HAVE HAD THE ADVICE OF INDEPENDENT LEGAL COUNSEL PRIOR TO ENTERING INTO THIS AGREEMENT AND DO SO VOLUNTARILY.

THIS AGREEMENT MAY BE MODIFIED ONLY IN WRITING, SIGNED BY BOTH PARTIES, DATED AND WITNESSED.

Dated this _____ day of _____, _____

Witnessed:

_____          _____
Attorney for Wife                            Wife

_____          _____
Attorney for Husband                      Husband

CHAPTER SIX

# SPOILS OF WAR: DIVIDING THE BOOTY

W hat is yours and yours alone when you are married? Is there anything that your spouse can't get in the divorce? The answer depends upon where you live, where the divorce is filed, and the proclivity of the judge assigned to your case.

## Community Property versus Marital Property

You have probably heard the term "community property" and may be aware that in nine states, primarily in the West, all community property is equally divided in a divorce proceeding. Everything else belongs to the individual partners. What is community property? An oversimplified definition is that any property acquired by the couple during the marriage is community property. Property owned before the marriage is not and remains the separate property of each partner. There are exceptions to this general rule, one of the most important of which is that the parties can agree in a pre- or postnuptial agreement to divide the community property in a different manner. In community property states, a major part of the battle will be in determining just what is and what is not community property. This is a battle for your lawyer and will not affect your planning. (Note that there are places in the United States where you must file a list of your claimed separate property in order for it not to be considered community pro-

61

perty. Your lawyer will take care of this for you if it is required in your state.)

The important point is to identify what types of things are subject to division by a divorce court so that you can get your fair share of those and keep those items that cannot be divided.

Unfortunately, for some people the list of things that a divorce court can't touch is shrinking fast. Once upon a time, a person's education was not a divisible asset. Nowadays, more and more states are allowing the value of a professional education to be considered in the total asset division. These laws were passed in response to cases like that of my old friend Larry.

He and his wife married just before Larry started law school. They had made a deal that she would work to put him through professional school and he would then do the same for her. While in his last year of law school, Larry confessed to me that he intended to divorce his wife as soon as he graduated. In the meantime, he maintained the fiction that the marriage was solid, using her hard work and good intentions to get his education. Just as he said, he did divorce her, and the law at that time did not allow her any property interest in his degree. She was what we lawyers call "without legal recourse."

Today, many courts in many states would put a value on her contribution to that education and make him pay it to her. The lesson here? If your spouse is in school and the marriage is in trouble, it might be a good idea (depending upon the law in your jurisdiction) to wait until the degree is awarded to file for divorce. Your property interest is then vested. Conversely, if you are the one in school, try to get divorced before graduation so that the property interest is not vested. The court can still take your education into account, but the fact that you have not yet graduated, and may not, means that the valuation of that education is much less.

The professional practice is another area where the law is expanding. A dental, medical, law, or even accounting practice is now being treated like any other business, with a value that can be assessed for property division purposes. In fact, there are people who do nothing but specialize in the valuation of these and other businesses. Much of their business comes from divorce lawyer referrals. If your spouse has a professional practice or any other business skill, it may be possible to put a value on it for purposes of negotiating a divorce property settlement. For instance, even a valuable specialized skill, such as that held by computer programmers, specially trained gourmet chefs, teachers, and even foreign-car mechanics could be considered a divisible asset even if the spouse did not assist in obtaining it. I would sure make the argument if my spouse had anything other than general employment and I did not.

To determine just what the value of an education is, trial lawyers use the professional opinion of experts specializing in valuing professional practices, businesses, and such. These experts put a price tag on the enhanced earnings potential of increased education and can give a present value for a professional practice as a going concern, thereby adding another asset to the total of the marital property to be divided. Some courts will only put a value on a degree beyond the bachelor's degree, but the argument is worth making that any advanced education is an asset.

## The Marital Home

The marital home is the primary asset owned by most couples. As a general rule, both parties own the house and, therefore, each has a property interest in it. However, the court does not have to divide it equally and does not have to do so right now. If there are minor children, it is not at all unusual to allow the custodial parent to keep possession of the house until the kids all reach the age of majority. The spouse gets a lien on the property but can't do anything with his or her share of the equity until the kids are grown. Keep in mind, though, that this is a general rule, not applicable in all states. In Mississippi, a "title" state, if the house is in the sole name of one person, the house is his; and in Texas, the courts protect the "homestead" from division in a divorce proceeding.

## Pension Plans

Another important marital asset is the pension plan. It has only been in the last fifteen or twenty years that a person has been found statutorily to have an interest in the spouse's pension plan. Now, thanks to state and federal laws, the spouse has a right to a share of the pension based upon the length of the marriage and the value of the pension as of the date of divorce. Note that this does not give you one-half of the total pension when your spouse retires (unless he is retiring soon or is already retired), and you generally do not get the money until your spouse would be eligible to get it himself. But you can have the value of your share determined and bargain to get it now as part of the total property division. You would be accepting a cash payment from your spouse in exchange for not claiming an interest in the pension later. This is potentially a very important part of your total settlement package.

There are three ways you can get your share of the pension. You can (1) take a cash payment now in exchange for your spouse keeping it all at the time of retirement; (2) you can wait until your spouse retires and get a share of the retirement at that time, or (3) you can get a qualified domestic relations order (QDRO), which will order the pension administrator to make your share of the pension benefits payable directly to you. Note, though, that there are exceptions to the QDRO law—not all types of pensions are subject to it.

## Previously Owned Property

What about things owned before the marriage? Keeping in mind that divorce judges pretty much do whatever they want with any of the property, in the non–community property states, those items generally belong to the person who owned them previously, and they are not part of the property to be divided. For example, suppose the wife owned stock in her own name before the marriage valued at $10,000. After a five-year marriage, she still owned the same stock and it had increased in value to $12,000. The stock is not part of the marital property and belongs to the wife. Only property acquired during the marriage is subject to division. But like everything else in the law, there are exceptions. The most important being that increases in the value of separately owned property are usually marital property. In the above example, the $2,000 increase could be considered a marital asset. Let me illustrate further.

John and Marie each owned homes when they married. Marie sold hers and moved into John's. Her name was not put on the title. Some of Marie's money went into fixing up John's house, some was spent on a honeymoon trip and various household expenses, and the balance was put into a joint account that they both used throughout the marriage, depositing and withdrawing money and mingling everything to the point that Marie's money could no longer be identified. During the ten years of marriage, the value of the house increased dramatically. When John filed for divorce, he told Marie that since the house was his before the marriage, it remained his and she had no interest in it at all. (He, of course, expected to divide everything else up equally.) John's position was reiterated by his attorney. Fortunately for Marie, she did not take his legal advice and retained her own lawyer, who convinced the court that John was entitled only to the approximate value of the house before the marriage, as his separate property. The increased value of John's house was split fifty-fifty. The judge also gave Marie additional money for using the proceeds of her house sale to improve the property—enough to compensate her for much of the lost profits on her house. Herein lies an important rule: There are no really firm rules in dividing property.

Some states even have statutes that are supposed to tell the judges how to divide up things. But all that the statutes actually do is tell the judge what to take into consideration when making the division. I will tell you a secret. Judges have their own way of looking at property division based upon their own feelings. They will be sure to say they have followed the statutory guidelines, but in the end will base their judgment on their own predispositions. One judge told me, off the record, that he always gives the marital home to the wife if there are very young minor children and she can afford to maintain it. Another said confidentially that she divides everything right down the middle unless one of the spouses was outrageously at fault (and I am in a no-fault state). Then, she would make it a sixty-forty or seventy-thirty split. Years ago, I had a judge refuse to give the wife the house, even though the husband was not fighting the divorce, was asserting no claim to the house, and even though I had filed all the required default papers to get the house for her. He took me into his chambers and said that he did not care what the state law said. He told me that he wanted the husband's in-court permission to give her the house or he would not do it. If I did not like it, I could appeal, which would have cost my client thousands of dollars. It was an inconvenience to bring the husband into court, but we were able to do it and get my client what she wanted. The point is that regardless of what the state law says, the judge can do whatever he or she wants. Thus, it is extremely important to get a lawyer who understands the local system and the judges (see chapter 8 for more information on lawyers).

### Inherited Property

Any property that you inherit usually remains yours even if you divorce. (I say "usually" because this rule is not true in every state.) But watch out for "commingling." If you put inherited money in with the other family assets and mix it all together, it may be difficult to determine whether you are spending your inheritance or spending the joint marital money. Of course, if your spouse inherits, it is in your interest to see that it is commingled. That way, you end up with a share of the inheritance anyway. Keep in mind, again, that the inherited property rule is not hard and fast; the judge can divide any property either of you owns, no matter how it was acquired, if he is so inclined.

### Hidden Assets

I mentioned earlier the man who converted his property to gold coins to keep it away from his wife. He did not get away with it, but a lot of people are successful in concealing assets. Remember that a judge can only divide what he knows about. And you can only ask for what you know about. (Refer to chapter 1 on keeping yourself informed of the family finances and keeping track of the paperwork and tax records.)

Generally though, if you are seeking a divorce, it is an excellent idea to show your attorney all tax records, canceled checks, bank statements, medical records for the family, and all statements from stockbrokers, mortgage companies, insurance and pension plans, and every other important-looking document you can lay your hands on. These can provide clues to assets you know about as well as hidden assets.

How do people hide assets? There are many ways, some of which make it difficult to track down the assets. Probably the most common tactic is putting it in someone else's name, usually a relative's. Surely Mom will be happy to keep a bank account for you, or let you use her safe-deposit box. She can get another key for you. But be careful to whom you give your things, even your own mother. You may not get them back.

I once had a civil case that dragged on for six years in the quagmire of the Wayne County court system in Detroit. On the advice of another attorney, a mother put all her extensive real-estate holdings into the names of her two adult daughters in addition to herself in order to avoid probate (there are much better ways to avoid probate, by the way). Everything was going fine until one of the daughters became involved in a divorce. The son-in-law claimed a property interest in the jointly owned property. We filed a legal action to invalidate the deeds. It took a lot of time and money to straighten out the mess, and in the end the son-in-law got a token settlement to prevent an appeal.

A bank account in another state usually works as a method to hide money since we lawyers do not usually look far from where the people work or live. We always file "interrogatories" (written questions asking about assets), but what if the other side does not fight the divorce, content with what he has hidden away? And if the defendant does not hire a lawyer to fight over the property, it can be difficult and expensive to interrogate him as to the assets.

The reason is that in court, where both sides have lawyers, there are specific rules and procedures that require both sides to answer all questions relating to their assets while under oath. If one side does not have a lawyer and is not a part of the proceedings, the process of getting him in to answer questions is more difficult and expensive. Certainly, he can be subpoenaed to appear for a deposition, but whether he can be found and if he will answer the questions truthfully are other matters. The prosecuting lawyer has to know what questions to ask and may not be able to sort the truth from the lies. It can be very difficult to trace bank accounts, bonds, securities, stocks, and other kinds of intangible assets. There is not always a paper trail. Keep informed as to your spouse's total income and where it goes.

Most states do not have one state registry listing all real estate owned and the names of the owners; each county keeps its own separate records. Therefore, any real estate a person's spouse owns is sometimes impossible to determine. We rely on our spouse to tell us when we ask. If they lie, there is little we can do. One thing to try is checking loan applications if you find them in the family financial paperwork; your spouse may have listed his assets to qualify for a loan. You can also look carefully at income tax returns to trace sources of income and deductions. There are services that will, for a fee, trace assets for you.

You only get one shot at the property settlement part of your divorce judgment. It is important that you know what all the assets are, and how the judge would treat certain types of property if the decision were hers. Before you enter into any final agreement, be certain that what you are agreeing to is what you are entitled to. Identifying hidden assets is part of this. The other part, if your goal is to get the largest possible property division, is getting the maximum amount of your spouse's premarital property and seeing that he gets the minimum amount of what you had coming into the marriage.

## List of Types of Marital Assets

A fire recently broke out in the building next to my law office. While our premises only suffered smoke and water damage, I was amazed at the list of property prepared by my insurance company. Every single pencil, book, and chair was itemized. I could never have remembered everything that was there had everything burned. I tell you this to introduce the following list. None of us can remember everything that we or our spouses might own. Use this list to identify the possible types of property you both have. It may help to catch something you otherwise would have missed and will be a valuable aid to you and your lawyer in arriving at a property settlement. There may be others, but these are the most common things to look for:

• Real estate, including rights to receive payments on property sold on contract or mortgage, jointly owned property, rights in time-shares, condominiums and cooperatives, leases on land or buildings, shares in real estate ventures; prepaid dockage or storage fees.

• Corporate stock, mutual funds, government or corporate bonds, brokerage accounts, investment contracts, futures or commodities accounts, investments in businesses, options, shares or percentages in oil, mining, or other joint ventures.

• Retirement, pension, Keogh, and IRA accounts; cash values of life insurance; tax-deferred annuities or employer-deferred bonuses and salary; accrued stock or certificate savings or profit-sharing account at employer; accrued vacation and sick pay; tax refunds.

• Bank accounts (joint accounts with another, foreign or numbered accounts, savings and checking accounts); certificates of deposit, shares in savings and loan companies; contents of safe-deposit boxes; cash on hand.

• Collections, such as stamps, coins, books, paintings, antiques, or other valuable collectibles.

• Automobiles, trucks, snowmobiles, motorcycles, boats, motors, aircraft, trailers, or recreational vehicles.

• Office equipment, furniture, instruments, cameras, computers, machinery, tools, jewelry, inventory, guns and other weapons; hunting, recreational, and sports equipment.

• Rights to sue or pending lawsuits or workers' compensation and disability cases; rights to inherit from an estate or trust where the interest is vested.

• Anything else of major value, including the wedding rings and jewelry. (I had a client whose husband had invested thousands of dollars in vitamins, which he had been attempting to sell door-to-door. He kept them in the garage and the wife took half the cases in the settlement.)

A judge will sometimes take a very pragmatic approach to dividing property. One judge I know has the parties list all the property of the marriage and their individual values. Then he goes down the list with a marking pen writing *H* or *W* on each item, trying to make an approximate equal value distribution.

It is very important that you list every item your spouse considers his so that it will be deducted from his share of the total. Do not forget those expensive golf clubs, the fishing boat, and the tools in the garage. Little things add up fast.

## Your Property Plan

To be certain that you receive your fair share of the marital property, you must do two things. The first, identifying all the marital property, you have already done. Now you have to develop good evidence to support your claim to your share of it all. You have to justify to the court what you want. A good plan will also aid you in achieving a favorable settlement without going to court. If your case is well prepared, your spouse may settle rather than face what he sees as an expensive and inevitable loss in court.

I have taken the eleven factors from the Illinois divorce law to use as an excellent basis for your property plan. Illinois has a comprehensive list of factors, which I believe to incorporate all the important points you would bring up in a trial supporting your property case. I have added "fault" as the twelfth factor since, even though Illinois does not allow fault to be considered in deciding property disputes, other states do (and even in those that don't, there is usually a way to let the judge know about the fault aspects of the divorce).

Use this plan as a guide to gathering and organizing your evidence for your lawyer. Do not be concerned with whether or not it is admissible as evidence. That is her job. Here are the factors that you will use to justify your claims:

- The contribution or dissipation of each party in the acquisition, preservation, or depreciation or appreciation in value of the marital and nonmarital property, including the contribution of a spouse as a homemaker or to the family unit.
- The value of the property set apart to each spouse. This refers to items that are not in dispute since both parties agree on their disposition.

- The duration of the marriage. It is likely that in a very short marriage the court will try to put each party back into the position they were in before the marriage. However, if you and your spouse lived together for an appreciable time before you married, be sure to tell your lawyer. You may be able to tack on this time to the length of the marriage for equitable reasons, using a sort of "palimony" argument.

- The relevant economic circumstances of each spouse when the division of property is to become effective, including the desirability of awarding the family home, or the right to live therein for reasonable periods, to the spouse having custody of the children.

- Any obligations and rights arising from a prior marriage of either partner. If you are already paying child support or alimony, that fact will be considered in determining how much more you will have to pay now.

- Any prenuptial agreement of the parties. This factor is useful only in those states that recognize the validity of premarital agreements—which, today, is the majority. If you signed one, show it to your lawyer. *Do not assume that a premarital agreement is always valid*, even if your state recognizes their validity. In many cases, the court can set them aside for reasons that include nondisclosure of assets or undue influence.

- The age, health, station, occupation, amount and sources of income, vocational skills, employability, estate, liabilities, and needs of each of the parties. Obviously, if there is a great disparity in earning ability between the spouses, it would be reasonable to award a greater share of the marital property to the lower-income spouse.

- The custodial provisions for any children. Some property may be given to the custodial parent just because it is necessary for the children's upbringing or care such as certain furniture and household goods and items necessary for using the family home.

- Whether the apportionment is in lieu of or in addition to maintenance. This refers to so-called lump-sum alimony. As I have already explained, alimony can be of three kinds: lump-sum, permanent, or temporary. Lump-sum is closely analogous to a property settlement since what you receive is a share of the marital property in exchange for giving up your alimony claim. You, in effect, receive a larger share of the marital property and give up any future claims for spousal support. It gives the person paying it certainty since there can be no later claim for an increase. The trend in the law is toward lump-sum and away from periodic payments. Discuss the types of alimony with your attorney to see if you qualify to receive it and what type would work best for you.

- The reasonable opportunity of each spouse for future acquisition of capital assets and income. Possible future inheritances and the likelihood of increasing income should be listed here. It may be that your spouse will have far greater economic opportunities in the future and, therefore, your share of the marital property should be larger.
- Whether the property was owned prior to the marriage or was acquired during the marriage and the source of the property. As I explained, if you owned it first and keep it separate during the marriage, you increase your chances of keeping it after the divorce.
- The respective fault of the parties in contributing to the breakdown of the marital relationship. Judges will sometimes, even without admitting it, use fault to punish the wrongdoer and reward the aggrieved party by adjusting the shares of property on each side.

This list can be used by your attorney as an outline of his presentation of your property plan to the court. You will need to find evidence, witnesses, or specific information to support each of the above factors.

The fact that property is held in only one name does not determine ownership in a divorce in most states. Mississippi and (for some types of property) Texas are exceptions. Regardless of what your spouse tells you, it is likely that you have an ownership interest in all property acquired during the marriage even if your name is not on it.

Note that a number of these factors relate to the respective economic circumstances of the parties. You may be entitled to a larger share of the property if you are unable to earn as much as your spouse now or in the future.

Use all the lists in this section and you are likely to be able to identify all property of the marriage as well as show the judge good reasons why you should get your fair share. Preparation of this kind is also invaluable in preparing your settlement offer to help you achieve your ultimate goal.

## Other Spoils of War

In the long run, alimony and child support payments often add up to more than the total of the marital assets. The levels of these are determined by the respective incomes of the spouses.

A new trend in the law is to base support and alimony not on the actual income, which can be manipulated, but on the ability to earn. The system calls this the "imputed income." For example, Marsha and Neil divorced and Neil remarried. Neil was a part-time instructor in a community college, and his child support payment was based upon that income. But Marsha wanted more when she discovered that Neil had been offered a full-time position but had turned it down. It seemed his new wife made enough money to support them both and he did not want the additional responsibility of a full-time job. Marsha was initially denied an increase, but had it granted on appeal. The court said that Neil's *ability to earn* should be the criteria for determining the level of support. He was forced to accept the full-time job since he was paying an amount of child support based upon his imputed income, that is, what he could be making.

Some courts are even assigning a value to various educational levels in setting minimum support amounts. The assumption is that a specific amount of education enables a person to earn a certain minimum income and, therefore, that person should be able to pay a certain minimum level of support. More education = more income = more support. This is true even if the person is actually unable to find work. I am not sure these assumptions are sound in today's economy—we have all heard the stories of underemployed or unemployed college graduates—but it is the law.

## Bargaining Over Support

Remember that if you and your spouse cannot agree, the court will set the support amount for you. But if you can agree, in some states the judge cannot interfere with the support level in your agreement. Find out from your attorney what the court-ordered support amount would be and bargain accordingly. Bargaining is involved in trying to reach an agreement on all the issues of the divorce. You may accept less support and more alimony or property. Ask your lawyer specifically whether the court ever approves more or less than a standard support amount and under what conditions it might do so. Sometimes you can get a different amount than the standard set by the state law by following specific statutory guidelines. But be careful if you are trying to buy your way out of child support.

Bart offered his wife Jessica 90 percent of the marital property if she would ask for a minimum level of support. Jessica agreed, but Bart's attorney told him that there was no way such an agreement could be made legally binding; it could not be put into the judgment since the judge could not legally approve bargaining away rights to child support, which belonged to the child, not the mother. Bart said, "Don't worry. I know my wife. A deal's a deal." The agreement was not put into the judgment.

Famous last words. Bart was right. He did know his wife. Jessica did not ask for any more child support when she had used up her divorce settlement. Instead, she went on public assistance. The district attorney representing the state Aid to Dependent Children Program filed a motion for an increase in support so that Bart not only lost his share of the marital property but ended up paying the regular amount of support anyway. The prosecutor's argument was, predictably, that the support was for the children, not the mother, and therefore she could not deal it away.

If you are Jessica, this tactic can work well for you; but if you are Bart, be careful of agreements that are not in writing.

## Promises versus Cash

You would be surprised how many people accept their spouse's word on promised future action rather than demanding their rights immediately, only to be disappointed when the ex-spouse does not follow through.

Terri and Mel were operating a laundromat and dry-cleaning store when they filed for divorce. Mel wanted to keep the store operating since it was his only way of making a living, and he did not want any liens on it since he said he needed its full value to use as collateral for his business loans. He made a deal with Terri that if she gave up all rights to the store, he would pay her $500 a month in cash "under the table" for five years. He planned on skimming the money from the store's cash receipts.

For the first year, Mel kept his word. Then the payments began coming late. Finally, he said he could not pay her anymore. There was nothing Terri could do. She had agreed to an illegal arrangement. The property settlement was fixed, in writing, and signed by the judge. And we know that property settlements are final unless we can prove fraudulent concealment. Terri and Mel's agreement was worth the paper it was not written on. Mel's cynical promise worked well for him. (See chapter 11 on getting revenge.)

## Income Taxes in Divorce

The tax laws change constantly so you should not rely on what I tell you as the final word on taxes. However, I do want to alert you to areas that you should discuss with your attorney since they may have tax ramifications. After consulting your attorney, ask him to give you a letter explaining all the tax aspects of your divorce settlement or judgment. This is important, first of all, as support for your tax deduction (the portion of your legal fees relating to tax advice is itself deductible), and second, if the attorney is wrong, the letter gives you documentary evidence upon which you can base a legal malpractice claim.

The seven issues with the most important tax consequences are:

### 1. Child support payments

Child support does not count as taxable income to the recipient nor is it deductible by the payer.

## 2. Alimony

*Permanent* alimony allows you to receive payments for the rest of your life or until a certain specified event occurs, such as remarriage. *Temporary* alimony is for a set number of years or months. It is similar to lump-sum alimony, since the total amount to be paid can easily be determined. Permanent alimony may be tax deductible to the payer and taxable to the recipient. Temporary alimony consisting of a fixed number of payments over less than ten years may not be deductible or taxable since it could be considered installment payments of lump-sum alimony. Lump-sum alimony is neither taxable nor deductible. This is an area that changes frequently. Before you enter into any alimony arrangement, be sure that you know the tax aspects.

Whatever your personal goal regarding alimony (pay the least/get the most), paying the least possible amount of taxes should be a priority. Therefore, discuss with your attorney a payment structure that maximizes the money that goes to the spouse and minimizes the amount of your money that goes to the IRS.

## 3. Property division

A very important part of your settlement negotiations should be an analysis of the tax consequences of a property split. For instance, if you transfer the marital home to your spouse in exchange for other property equal to the equity you would be giving up, a taxable gain may result. You may have to pay income taxes on the amount of the value of the equity you receive. You may be able to defer this tax by reinvesting, but that may not be possible. The Taxpayer Relief Act of 1997 gives you a large exemption from this capital gains tax but you may still be in a taxable position depending upon the amount of the gain. (Remember, the law changes continually, so get current advice.) Taxes can also be triggered by other asset transfers, such as appreciated stocks. Again, ask your lawyer about the tax consequences of every aspect of your divorce. If you go to trial because you were unable to settle, have your accountant testify as to the consequences of various transfers since the tax consequences should be taken into consideration by the judge.

**4. Filing status**

Your marital status on December 31 is what counts. If your divorce is final by then, you are considered divorced for the entire year and can only file as single (or as head of the household if you have a minor child living with you). You may not file as married filing jointly or as married filing separately. Similarly, if you are not legally divorced by the end of the year, even though a divorce is ongoing and you are separated, you may not file as a single person.

So, if your divorce is nearing settlement at the end of the year, you may be able to choose whether you want to be divorced this year or next year. Analyze the tax consequences of each option and plan accordingly. Filing status can be a powerful tool in negotiations. If one spouse has a higher income and is counting on being able to file jointly to minimize taxes, the other spouse can refuse to file jointly as a bargaining chip. On the other hand, if you are the one counting on filing jointly, you might consider getting the tax return signed before you file for divorce.

**5. Dependency exemptions**

Generally, the law is that the person with custody gets the exemptions. Do not claim the exemption on your taxes if you are not legally entitled to it. The IRS now requires the social security numbers of every dependent claimed, so you are very likely to be caught if you both try to claim the same child.

## 6. Refund checks

If a joint tax refund is coming, it is wise to have it sent directly to your attorney. Although it is illegal, it is not uncommon for one spouse to keep the entire check, even forging the spouse's name on it for deposit. It is difficult to do anything about that.

## 7. Legal fees

Your own attorney's fees are deductible to the extent they were incurred for tax planning and advice, subject to severe limitations set by the IRS (which seem to change frequently). Payment of your spouse's legal fees is not generally deductible. Get an itemized breakdown of the tax portion of your legal fees, then ask your accountant how much of it you can deduct.

# CHAPTER SEVEN

# WEAPONS

All the resources you have available to put forward the best case possible are your weapons. These are the tools you use to achieve your ultimate goal of getting what you really want. Money is one of the most effective weapons in your arsenal. You can use it offensively, by either buying your way out of the marriage or by paying your attorney to maintain a complex and costly pretrial and trial proceeding. Defensively, you can ask for money controlled by your spouse or force him to spend money he does not want to spend.

This option is very common and might be called a war of attrition: make him pay and pay and pay. Your objective in most divorce proceedings is to force a settlement that gives you what you really want without actually going to trial. Sometimes it will be necessary to force your opponent to see that giving you what you want is also the best thing for him to do. And one way to do that is to wear him down with the legal process.

It is very expensive to maintain a contested divorce case. Attorney fees add up very quickly. There are a number of things your lawyer can do to increase the cost and complicate the proceedings. Ethically, a lawyer cannot intentionally try to drag out a case, but you can request that he do the most thorough job possible for you. This might mean, for instance, that instead of submitting written questions to the other side to prepare his case, your lawyer could hold depositions. In other words, he could require each witness to appear in person to answer his questions, before trial and under oath. Depositions are expensive for both sides because they take many hours, during which both attorneys must be present and a court reporter has to be paid to record and transcribe the questions and answers.

You can see that if you have the money to spend, you can sometimes force a settlement by making the proceedings so expensive that settling will be an attractive alternative. It is not that you are trying to force an unfair settlement, you are simply using this tactic to force a partner who is refusing to discuss settlement at all to be more reasonable.

If you do not have money but your spouse does, you can ask the court to make him pay your attorney fees so that you can maintain the case. It is not at all unusual; in fact, payment of the other side's attorney fees is an issue in nearly every contested case. Most judges will grant some amount of attorney fees to the spouse who cannot afford to pay for the proceedings as a matter of fundamental fairness. Your spouse will then be paying for both lawyers. At the prices we lawyers charge nowadays, it won't take long until he seeks settlement.

This works particularly well if his objective is financial and yours is not, such as when you are trying to get the children and your spouse is working for a bigger share of the property. You can use up a good share of the marital property by refusing to settle on anything but your own terms. Your objective—the children—is still there, while his—the money—is being used up.

## Court Orders

Interim court orders are very effective weapons in a variety of instances. Divorce courts are called "equity courts" from the old English system, on which our legal system is based. In the old system, there were courts of law and courts of equity. It used to be that if you failed to get satisfaction in the law court, which was under the authority of the king, you could appeal to the equity court, under the authority of the church, to intervene and do the right thing. Equity means fairness.

Divorce courts are empowered to do what the judge thinks is fair, within the bounds of the written law. Therefore, you will see many shoot-from-the-hip decisions by divorce judges. A judge can do whatever he or she thinks is fair under the circumstances, even if neither party agrees with the decision nor asked for the particular remedy the court is imposing.

Motion day in divorce court is almost like watching *The People's Court* on television. Divorce motions are filed for nearly every kind of temporary relief imaginable. Following are some examples of real motions I have heard or filed myself.

### Temporary Support
In addition to asking the court to set child support levels during the time the divorce is in progress, you can request specific additional payments. I have had clients request payment of private school tuition, special tutoring, money for braces and orthodontics, all kinds of things. Those paying support may come to the judge to request credit for the time the kids were with him on vacation; to ask that the support levels be reduced because of his reduced income; and even to complain that the support money is being spent on his wife's boyfriend and not on the children.

Judges make decisions in these instances quickly, based on their own notions of fairness. Generally, the decisions are made without taking testimony, allowing cross-examination or the other niceties of regular court procedure. Judges often rely solely on the unproven statements of the opposing lawyers; and they may change their minds a few weeks later if the same matter is again brought to their attention.

### Temporary Custody
Temporary custody is always a potential issue for a court order. I had a client whose husband filed a motion for a change in temporary custody every two or three weeks based on "new evidence" he said he had discovered about my client. He complained, among other things, that she smoked too much around the kids, that her boyfriend was sleeping over, that she left them with a baby-sitter too often, that she used prescription drugs excessively, that the children were doing

poorly in school, that she did not feed them adequately so that they went to school hungry, that their clothing was dirty when he picked them up . . . it went on and on. Most of the charges were baseless or exaggerated, but he had a right to ask for relief and the costs skyrocketed. He could have put all his allegations down on one petition, but instead brought them up one at a time just to frustrate my client and complicate the proceedings.

### Restraining Orders and Injunctions

During the months that it takes for a case to get to trial, it is sometimes necessary to ask for the court's help to make your spouse either do or stop doing something. For example, assault injunctions order him not to strike or harm you and can even stop him from seeing you, calling you on the telephone, or coming near your workplace or home. While, of course, it is against the general criminal laws to assault anyone, including your spouse, the assault injunction puts the additional civil contempt power of the court behind the order. This is important because to convict someone in a criminal court, the offense must be proven beyond a reasonable doubt. In a civil contempt situation, all your lawyer has to show is that it is more likely than not your spouse violated the court order. To obtain an assault injunction, you need to say that you have a real fear of being harmed in some way. Domestic assault laws in many jurisdictions make getting the assault injunction quite easy.

There are courts where injunctions against assault are entered automatically in all cases, and they are effective against both marital partners. The rationale is that anyone objecting to such an order must be planning on violating it. Those that are automatically entered do not, of course, include the provisions against telephoning and visiting the workplace, and do not interfere with the legal rights of visitation with the minor children.

A restraining order can be issued to stop your spouse from using up the marital assets. You can have a freeze put on the bank accounts so that only the court can authorize withdrawals. She can be ordered not to transfer, borrow against, give away, or sell anything. You can really tie things up just on the premise that you are afraid she is going to waste the marital property that is presumably partly yours. The only defense she can offer to your request for an injunction is that she is not going to do what you say she is. If she really isn't, then there is no reason not to have the injunction.

Injunctions are good tools primarily because of the enforcement power the court has to back them up. If your spouse violates a court order, the judge can issue an "Order to Show Cause," which requires him to appear before the judge to explain his failure to follow the order. The judge can then jail him immediately and indefinitely without any trial by invoking another weapon, contempt of court.

### Contempt of Court

What if the judge enters an order but your spouse violates it? He can be declared by the judge to be in contempt of court. This status allows the judge to have him jailed either to punish him for the violation or to force him into compliance. Once you get a court order, you have substantial power. Later on, we will talk more about the importance of being the one to file the divorce, but a point needs to be made here.

When you initiate the divorce, the court commonly will enter, at your request, standard form orders that can give you temporary custody, order your spouse to pay temporary support (sometimes even temporary alimony and attorney fees), and even temporary injunctions against assault and transfers of property. To get these, you must fill out information forms and sometimes sworn affidavits detailing the current status of you, your spouse, and the children. There are parameters and guidelines used by the court to determine what types of orders are appropriate in a given case. Once these orders are in effect, they have the force of law. If he wants them changed, he must hire an attorney, file a motion, and ask the judge to change them. He is on the defensive and better have good reasons to justify changing an order already in existence. You, as the filing plaintiff, had to make only general allegations and satisfy the criteria listed in state law and local rules to get your orders. It puts you in the driver's seat with the power of contempt of court backing you up. You are in a terrific position to begin settlement negotiations.

## Discovery

"Discovery" is a legal term meaning the process by which we find out everything that we need to know to carry on our case. For example, with discovery you have a legal right to see and have copies of all your spouse's financial records. Things you always wanted to know are now available to you. During a deposition, your lawyer is allowed to ask your spouse, in your presence, anything he or she likes, whether or not it is admissible at trial, so long as it is relevant to the divorce. And in a divorce, nearly anything can be relevant. Your spouse must answer under oath. If he will not, then you can file a motion in court to have the judge compel him to answer.

Want to find out about extramarital affairs, with names, places, and dates? How about some shady business deals you think he was involved in? Has he earned any money under the table that has not been reported on his tax returns? Has there ever been any criminal record? What were the details? What about drug use, now or in the past? All these things can be asked and he must answer truthfully or he has made a false swearing, which is illegal and punishable by fine or imprisonment.

Another potentially important point: if you request a written transcript of his testimony, it can become part of the public court record. Anyone can look at it, even years from now, leaving the potential for public humiliation and embarrassment.

The mere threat of being deposed and asked sensitive questions can cause a person to give concessions in settlement. Is doing so extortion? Or is it just good bargaining? I suppose it depends upon how you present it to your spouse.

The real value of discovery is in the information that can be obtained by your attorney. You will know in advance all the witnesses your spouse will use and what each will say. All the financial data will be available ahead of time, including the values of businesses, pension and retirement plans, employee benefit plans, and details on all investments. The attorney who does not conduct thorough discovery is not only doing you a big disservice, but is also committing malpractice.

## The Girlfriend (or Boyfriend)

Surprisingly, the girlfriend is often one of your strongest allies in getting you what you really want. The reason is that her objective is different from your spouse's. She really wants the whole mess to be done with so that she can begin a blissful relationship uncluttered by the ongoing divorce. She does not want your husband spending his money on the divorce and his energy worrying about it. She just wants him.

Unless the court says otherwise, there is nothing wrong with your contacting the girlfriend to discuss settlement of the case. At best, you might find out what your husband is willing to settle for. At worst, she will know you are interested in settling but are prepared to drag the divorce out as long as necessary to get what you want. She can put pressure on him that may be far more effective than anything you can do. The woman is not ever likely to be your best friend, so you have nothing to lose by trying. (Actually, I have seen cases where the ex-wife and the new wife did become good friends and remained so even after the spouse moved on to his third wife.)

## Espionage

In every war, covert intelligence gathering is common, if not indispensable. Knowing what the other side is planning and doing can be very helpful to your case. If the issues warrant the expense, a private investigator can help track down hidden income and assets, establish fault, and provide specific information on your opponent's personal habits that could be of use to you in trial or settlement negotiations.

### Surveillance

Some people actually plant bugs in the homes and cars of their spouses. I suppose they are hoping to collect usable information for their divorce trials. I have had people bring me tapes of the telephone conversations of their spouses, hoping that I will show them to the judge so he can see just how much of a jerk the spouse really is. Be careful. In some cases it is illegal to secretly tape someone's conversations. Although you may indeed find usable information, the risk of prosecution is not worth what you might gain. The way around this is to say right on the tape that the conversation is being record-ed. If your spouse continues to talk, she is implicitly consent-ing to the taping. Incidentally, I recently read another lawyer's divorce book that actually suggested making illegal tapes of conversations. Watch where you get your advice.

One client actually broke into her husband's house and went through his safe to get copies of his financial records. It worked for her, but if she had been caught she could have gone to jail. On the other hand, if the house is also yours and there are no court orders forbidding it, you can legally break into it—even if your spouse has had the locks changed.

### Spies

Neighbors of your spouse, if they were once your neighbors, can help you with some information gathering. You may find out whether he leaves the children home alone, who visits the home, and when or whether he has had overnight "guests." They can also tip you off if he starts moving away with all the furniture.

It is unfortunately all too common that the children are used as spies. Don't think you are being slick quizzing the kids. They catch on pretty quickly to the fact that you are putting them in the middle of your divorce problems and soon stop revealing information. Besides, do you really want your children to feel torn between you and your spouse, on top of the grief they are already feeling over the breakup of their family? Children should not be used as weapons. You have probably heard this before, but remember that the chil-dren are not the ones getting a divorce. Do not put them in the middle of it and make them casualties of war. There are plenty of other tactics you can employ without using them.

# CHAPTER EIGHT

# HIRED GUNS: LAWYERS

**D**o you necessarily need a lawyer? How do you find one who really knows divorce? How do you get one that you can trust? Should you have a male or female lawyer? These and many more questions plague people involved in divorce. First, let's address the question of whether you need a lawyer at all.

If your spouse has already filed for divorce, you should see a lawyer immediately, no matter what assurances you get from your spouse, to discuss your legal rights and obligations under the laws of your state. Find out what you stand to gain by being represented. You will not be sorry. Your spouse may tell you that she is seeking a no-fault divorce and you do not need a lawyer. Her lawyer will do it all. Do not rely on this. Get some independent, competent legal advice. A lawyer can represent only one side of the case, and if your spouse files first, the lawyer is obligated to protect her interests, not yours.

There are three specific circumstances in which you should always be represented by your own lawyer: (1) if you have minor children, (2) if either or both of you have substantial property, or (3) if your spouse is employed and you are not.

If you have minor children, I recommend that you get a lawyer to handle your case, even if you and your spouse are miraculously in complete agreement on custody. In my experience, when there are children, the divorce will become contested in one way or another before the statutory waiting period has expired 75 percent of the time. If you have seen a lawyer and you are the plaintiff (the one who filed for the divorce), then you are already represented, while your spouse has to go out and hire a lawyer of his own if he wants to fight you. Even if you both plan on the divorce being uncontested, be the plaintiff so that you are in the driver's seat (and if it starts out as uncontested, ask your spouse to give you half the attorney's fee).

You need to know that the agreement you have made with your spouse adequately covers all your rights and that you are not agreeing to substantially less than that to which you are legally entitled. Those with substantial property need to know whether they are agreeing to accept less than what the court would give them in a contested case. Those who are not working need to be advised of their rights to temporary or permanent alimony and whether their spouse's business or profession is part of the marital property.

It is too often the case that one spouse (usually the husband) is dominant and controlling and the other gets shortchanged in their informal agreement. If you are the spouse being victimized, a lawyer will recognize an attempt to rip you off. However, if you are the one who has gotten your spouse to agree to less than he is entitled to, the lawyer will put it all in legal form and put it through the courts so that it has the force of law. Remember that although your lawyer can't say it to your husband, you can tell him he does not need a lawyer. If he wants to take legal advice from you, that is fine. Also keep in mind that it is fairly common for spouses to lie about what the lawyer told them.

If you have no children, no property to speak of, and there is no demand or claim for alimony, you may be able to do the divorce yourself. It is basically just a matter of filling out the proper forms and filing them in the right place at the right time. In most areas of the country, women's rights groups and other organizations even sell divorce kits with all the paperwork and step-by-step instructions. Appendix A provides a list of online companies that will prepare your forms for you via the Internet.

However, if your spouse has served you with divorce papers, go see a lawyer immediately—no matter what assurances you get from your spouse. At least get the benefit of the lawyer's advice. You will not be sorry.

## Finding a Lawyer

Let's say you have made a deal with your spouse. You have decided to go for a "trial separation" and have agreed on the points that will go into a separation agreement. Now you need a lawyer to put it all into legal form. Where do you go?

First of all, you want to find a lawyer who specializes in divorce. The fact is that any lawyer is legally allowed to file a divorce action whether or not he has ever done so in the past. I suppose any surgeon could legally do brain surgery too, but would you want your podiatrist doing that job for you? Get a specialist. Again, you will not be sorry. Some states even certify lawyers as specialists in matrimonial or family law. Ask about certification.

It may not be a bad idea to have a paid conference with several divorce specialists before you hire one to represent you. Once a lawyer has discussed the divorce with you, he is not ethically allowed to represent your spouse. You can therefore narrow your husband's choice of attorneys by seeing the best ones first. I had a friend whose husband saw nearly every attorney in a small town about his intent to divorce—nearly thirty of them—forcing the spouse to go to the next town to get representation. The lawyer you choose will be involved in the most intimate and important decisions you make in your life and it is important that you find someone with whom you feel comfortable and confident.

If you don't really need a lawyer but don't want to fool around with the paperwork, one of the lawyers advertising budget divorces in the newspaper or yellow pages will probably work just fine for you.

But what if you need an advocate for your case? How do you find a good specialist? Well, the lawyers all know who they are, so why not ask a lawyer? Look in the yellow pages under "Attorneys." Pick the names of attorneys who are advertising specialties other than divorce. Call several and ask for a referral to a divorce specialist. After a few calls, one or more names will begin to be repeated. These are the people considered by other lawyers to be divorce specialists.

Another way is to pick the biggest firm you can find, the one with the most lawyers. Chances are that it has an attorney on staff who specializes in divorce. With a large firm you also get big resources and generally good management so that you can be confident that your case is being cared for adequately.

Referrals from friends are like playing the lottery: maybe you will get a good one and maybe not. Picking the lawyer with the biggest advertisement in the yellow pages will probably get you someone who does a high-volume, uncontested divorce business, but not necessarily someone who is really skilled in handling contested cases.

Regardless of who you pick, go into your first meeting armed with plenty of questions and get to know the attorney a bit before you hire him to handle your case. Here are some questions you should be sure to ask when you arrive at the conference:

• How many contested divorce cases have you actually handled?
• How many are you handling right now?
• How many contested custody cases have you done?
• How many have you won?
• How long have you been in practice in the area?
• What do you know about the local judges?
• Do you have a feeling for how they rule in various areas of divorce?

Don't worry about embarrassing the lawyer or yourself. Make sure that you are satisfied with the answers you get. This is your life that you are going to be dealing with, not his. The information you are asking for is not confidential and there is no reason why he should not tell you. Do not be afraid to get up and leave if the lawyer is evasive or tries to steer you away from your list of questions.

What about gender? Is it better to have a male or a female lawyer? I think there is no difference. The most important factors are the personality and training of the lawyer. How do you feel with this person? If you feel more comfortable with one than the other, then let that be your guide.

Sometimes the divorce is started in a town other than the one in which you live, in which case I recommend that you get a local attorney in that town to handle your case. An out-of-town lawyer—i.e. one from where you live—will be at a distinct disadvantage. Local attorneys know the judges. They are usually all members of the same local bar association. They may even play golf together. More importantly, they practice in the local courts and know what to expect from each judge. Out-of-town attorneys do not have that advantage. In some small towns there is even an unspoken prejudice against out-of-town lawyers.

The value of an attorney experienced in the court you will be using is in his familiarity with the judges. An experienced divorce attorney can almost predict what a given judge will do in most circumstances. I know of judges who do not approve of divorce cases run as "negative campaigns." They will punish lawyers who dwell on marital fault rather than on the merits of their own case. This predisposition is not written down anywhere. Only attorneys who have practiced in front of them a lot know that they feel this way.

You should also make sure that the attorney is well regarded by the court. This can be difficult to determine, but one thing you can do is get a look at your attorney in action before you hire him. Ask him when he will next be in court on a trial or motion, and attend the hearing. Court proceedings are open to the public. Go watch and see how he does. This can be very revealing. You can see his demeanor. Does he seem unprepared? Does he speak clearly, logically, and persuasively? How does he respond to the questions raised by the judge or the opposing counsel? How does he compare to the other attorneys in court that day?

## Working with Your Attorney

Now that you have picked your lawyer, you have to know how to handle him or her. The most important rule to remember is that the lawyer is working for you. You are the boss.

If you want to settle your case, your lawyer cannot stand in your way. Similarly, your lawyer may not make any deals with the other side without your approval. This sounds simple and obvious, but you would be surprised how much influence against your wishes a lawyer can exert.

Steve came to see me to represent him in the divorce action filed by his wife Jennifer. She had obtained an order for temporary custody and support and was staying in the marital home. Steve was not asking for anything unusual. He wanted joint custody with an even property split and had begun paying child support even before she filed her case.

Steve had made an appointment with me to discuss a settlement he said he and Jennifer had worked out between them. When he arrived in the office, however, he was upset.

"The deal is off," he said. "Jennifer and I had everything worked out. She would stay in the house until it was sold. Her brother, who is a real estate agent, was going to list it, then we would split the money down the middle."

"That sounds reasonable to me," I said, "so what's the problem?"

"Her lawyer. Jenny told me that her lawyer won't let her go through with the deal. He told her he is going ahead with the trial and she will get more that way."

"Does she want more now than what you agreed upon?" I asked.

"No. She says she still wants to settle but that her hands are tied. The lawyer won't let her do it."

One of two things was happening here. Either Jennifer was telling the truth, and her lawyer really said he would not let her go through with the settlement, or she was using the lawyer-as-scapegoat ploy.

I understand that often it is easier to blame everything on the lawyer to avoid arguing over the issues with your spouse. I even recommend it if your spouse is the argumentative and controlling type. It is a low-key way to avoid trouble. "My lawyer says I can't do it" is an easy way out of difficult discussions.

However, if what Jennifer said was true and she was not using the scapegoat trick, then something could be done. I said, "Steve, I cannot get involved in your wife's relationship with her attorney, but I can tell you that I work for you. If you tell me that you want to settle on certain terms, I can advise you against it if I think it is not in your best interest, but, ultimately, the final decision is yours and yours alone. I am required to settle your case the way you want—even against my advice. If I refuse to do it, you have the right to fire me or I can ask to be released from the case. Your wife has the same right."

Steve took it upon himself to advise his wife of her rights. She insisted upon the agreed settlement and the case was final within two weeks.

The lawyer can only advise. The decisions are yours to make. If your lawyer refuses to follow your wishes, fire him and find another one. However, you should feel very confident that you are making a good decision and that the advice you are getting from your present lawyer is wrong.

In general, I advise against replacing your lawyer in the middle of the proceedings unless there is some very compelling reason. First of all, the expense goes up, since the new lawyer will charge you for the time it takes to familiarize himself with the case. More importantly, it is sometimes difficult to find a good substitute attorney. I am always wary of someone who wants me to take over a case from another lawyer, so I am very careful about accepting it. I still remember the warning I received from a law professor during my first year of law school:

"Watch out for the insane people," he advised. "You young folks probably don't believe me, but when you get out and practice, you will see. There are a lot of crazy people going around hiring lawyers to do their fighting for them. They will cause you nothing but trouble and you will soon learn to steer clear of them."

He was right—especially with regard to divorce cases. Certain people do become a little crazy. Some are emotionally fragile to begin with, and the high stress levels associated with the breakdown of the marriage and the battles over custody, support, and property literally drive them over the edge. They go from lawyer to lawyer, trying to find one who can achieve the impossible goals they have set for themselves. If you change lawyers more than once, you will find it increasingly difficult to get adequate representation. Be selective the first time.

## Stirring Up the Mud

"Stirring up the mud" is a practice in which a few sleazy divorce lawyers engage. It is not the norm, but not all that uncommon either. What they do is take every minor complaint or disagreement and exaggerate it. They file volumes of paper with the courts and have court hearings over matters that could just as easily be settled with a telephone call. This is not the same as using the power of money to wear down the other side. This type of attorney will use this tactic on all his cases. He is merely building up his fee rather than watching out for the best interests of his client.

I once dealt with an old-time attorney, now retired, who refused to settle a dispute over visitation until we were in the hallway outside the courtroom, waiting for our case to be called. I remember the conversation:

"So we can just put the agreement in writing and have the judge sign it later, right?" I said.

He was peeking through the window of the courtroom, looking for his client. He spotted her and waved.

"Oh no," he said, shuffling his armload of files as he opened the door to the courtroom. "First, we have to argue about it on the record."

My confusion must have been apparent.

"Got to put on a show for the clients, you know," he added as he winked, nudged me, and walked through the door.

His behavior was, in my opinion, unethical and, in fact, if it could be proven, might even be considered malpractice. Watch out for lawyers who want to take every single thing to court. Sometimes just a telephone call from your lawyer to the other lawyer will get the problem solved without the considerable expense of a court hearing.

## Legal Malpractice

Malpractice is an area of the law that can sometimes work to your benefit. If your lawyer has failed to adequately represent you, it may be possible to collect monetary damages from him in a malpractice action. Malpractice can be something as simple as not conducting discovery in a contested property case. Just because you lose does not mean it was your lawyer's fault—but it might mean that. If you have lost significantly, it would not hurt to have the case file looked at by a legal malpractice lawyer (they advertise in the yellow pages). Unlike doctors, lawyers seem to have no reluctance at all to sue each other.

You can also file a complaint with the bar association if your lawyer has screwed up your case. Every year, hundreds of lawyers take on divorce cases and either do not handle them properly or do not do them at all! I see in my *Bar Journal* reports of lawyers accepting retainers and not filing the case, then lying about it; failing to file paperwork in sufficient time to avoid getting the case dismissed; forging their client's signatures on documents; and many other offenses. Now, before all the lawyers get mad at me, I want to make it clear that these are exceptions. Most lawyers are honest, competent, and have only the best interests of their clients at heart. But remember, if something seems to have gone seriously wrong with your case, you do not simply have to take your lawyer's word for what happened.

## Keeping Track of Your Case

I follow the practice, as do some other attorneys, of sending my clients copies of every paper and letter I prepare for them. My client then has a complete case file and knows exactly what I did for the fee I am charging. Many lawyers do not do this as a matter of course, but will if you insist upon it. *Insist upon it.* Tell your lawyer that if you do not get a copy of it, you are not paying for it. You will get the copies.

### Legal Fees

Legal fees are expensive—but then, so are those of plumbers, dentists, and auto mechanics. The most expensive attorney in town is not necessarily the best, and the least expensive is not usually the worst. The hourly rate does seem to go up with the years of experience, but I always remember what a prospective employer told me when I was job-hunting between college and law school. He said there is a big difference between ten years' experience and one year's experience repeated ten times over. Years in practice do not necessarily make the best lawyer.

Fees will almost always be on an hourly basis. You will be billed for every telephone call and letter written or read by your lawyer as well as time spent on research, depositions, document preparation, and interviews. The lawyer may also charge you for the time spent by legal assistants on your case (at a lower hourly rate). Rates vary depending upon the attorney involved and the area of the country.

There are no contingent fees in divorce cases. Your attorney is not able to charge based on a percentage of what you get, although you can agree to defer payment until you receive your settlement. Closely akin to contingent fees are "final fees," which are legally proper, but, in my mind, simply a slippery way around the contingent fee prohibition. Some attorneys in certain parts of the country ask for a performance bonus, something they call a "final fee," which is paid after the case is over. This is over and above the hourly fee already paid to them. Their justification is that if the outcome was especially good, they should be rewarded. I don't buy this argument and think these fees are uncalled for. It is the attorney's job to do the best he can for you. The only justification I can see for a fee like this (which can exceed the total hourly fees) is if the attorney also agrees to a rebate of fees to you if he does not get as good a deal as he might have gotten—then it's fair. In any case, this fee cannot be legally collected unless provisions are made for it in the fee agreement.

### Get a Written Fee Agreement

It is very important to get a written fee agreement that spells out exactly what you will be charged and the hourly rate. (See appendix D for one form of a fee agreement.) If you have been promised a flat fee, get it in writing. You will almost always have to pay a retainer to hire the lawyer. This is a deposit you make with her from which the billable hours and costs are charged. After the retainer has been used up, you will be asked to pay an additional retainer. The amount will be much higher for a case expected to be contested than for one that is not, since the attorney will base the amount on what she perceives will be the ultimate amount of time spent on the case.

### Insist upon Itemized Billings

You should not pay a bill that just says "for services rendered" or that gives a flat number of hours. Every letter, telephone call, court appearance, and conference should be itemized with the date of service and the amount of time being charged. You should insist on receiving an updated statement every month. You do not want to be surprised with a huge bill at the end of the case. You should know exactly how charges are accruing as your case is going along and how quickly your retainer is being used up.

I have already touched on the subject of having your spouse pay your fees. In most jurisdictions the court has the authority, and indeed a policy, of requiring a working spouse to assist in paying the attorney fees of a nonworking spouse. Sometimes there is a minimum amount that will automatically be ordered just by asking. Greater amounts may require a hearing in front of a judge, who will ask for specific reasons you need the assistance.

Attorney fees are part of the total settlement package. You should try and find out how much your spouse has paid his attorney if he is opposed to paying for yours. In a number of cases I was able to get the spouse to pay a good part of the attorney fees, even without a court order specifically requiring it.

Kathy retained me for full representation in the divorce started by her husband. He had paid a large retainer to his attorney and she was concerned that she could not afford the legal costs of a contested divorce suit. There were substantial marital assets, with a house, stocks, and a mutual fund account, but she had very little ready cash since her income was far less than that of her husband. I filed a motion in court to have the stocks and mutual funds put into an escrow account from which attorney fees for both sides would be paid. The court granted the motion and the husband's attorney did not fight too hard to stop me since his additional fees would also come from the account.

How did this strategy benefit my client? The mutual fund was a jointly owned asset. In the final settlement, what was left was split equally. The husband, in effect, paid for a portion of Kathy's attorney fees since he had already paid most of his own lawyer's fees from his own pocket, while all of hers were taken from the joint account.

Fees for a contested case are expensive. A properly prepared and tried divorce case, especially one involving custody, can easily cost thousands of dollars. In addition to attorney fees, there are discovery and deposition costs. We may hire psychologists, accountants, actuaries, and other expensive witnesses to help get ready for trial. Settlement, discussed in the next chapter, is almost always a good idea—so long as you get what you really want.

CHAPTER NINE

# PEACE TREATIES: SETTLEMENT

Settling is almost always better than going to trial.
Settling is almost always better than going to trial.

Settling is almost always better than going to trial.

By now you have figured out that I think settling is almost always better than going to trial. As long as you get what you really want, it is always better. Why? Several reasons.

Settling means the case can be finalized at once. No more delays. You are divorced once and for all. You have been spared the emotional trauma involved in a lengthy trial. Sometimes the very fact that a trial has been held exacerbates the rift between the two spouses such that they become life-long enemies, a terrible situation when they have minor children. In extreme cases, parties have even had emotional breakdowns caused by the high stress of the divorce trial.

Another very important consideration is that a settlement spares the children the pain of a custody battle. In many jurisdictions the preference of the child as to custody is a factor that must be taken into account by the judge. Even if the child is interviewed privately in the judge's office, it puts a terrible psychological burden on the child to have to express a preference between two parents that she may love equally.

Certainty is another reason to settle. The old "bird in the hand" theory has a lot going for it. You are going to be happier with your divorce if you have helped negotiate it than you might be if the judge makes all the decisions for you. While it is true that we attorneys can have a pretty good idea how the judge is going to decide a particular case, there are no guarantees. One of my favorite sayings is, Never make promises based upon what someone else is supposed to do. On the day of your trial the judge may not be in a good mood. Maybe she just had a fight with her husband, or her ulcer is acting up, or she is worried about her son dropping out of college. Your case is most important to you. To everyone else it is just another case. The average family court will process thousands of cases per year. They do not all go to trial, but a lot do. Try and settle so that you have the maximum possible input into the final result.

Judges can get impatient if they have to divide every single item of property and sometimes make decisions neither partner will like. I saw a judge express his frustation by dividing everything exactly equally, no matter what the item of property. The first eight volumes of the encyclopedia set went to the wife, the last eight to the husband. Half the husband's golf clubs went to the wife. Every set of draperies was divided in half. When he was through announcing his decision, the judge told the stunned couple to come back in a week if they could agree on a better plan. They came back with a settlement. Judges like settlements and for that reason are anxious to make settlement agreements stick.

Money, of course, is another reason to settle. Divorce trials can cost thousands of dollars more in attorneys fees than settling the case. Do you have that much more to gain by going to trial? Are you sure?

Most experienced divorce lawyers are good negotiators because negotiation and settlement is how the bulk of their cases are resolved. There is a fine art to negotiating. In fact, its subtleties are the subjects of dozens of books and colleges even have courses on the process. I will touch briefly on some key negotiating tactics.

First, I must reiterate: *do not reveal what you really want.* If your opponent knows what you have to have, then you will not get any more than that. Just as an old-fashioned horse trader would not immediately reveal the lowest price he would accept, you must not give away your true objective.

## Be Prepared to Compromise

Naturally, do not compromise your bottom line. Do negotiate those extras that you can live without. If, for example, you really want sole custody of the child, you can negotiate over property and alimony and even make major concessions in visitation, but do not accept any joint custody arrangement that will give you less than you have to have.

## Know Your Opponent

Make an educated guess as to what your spouse really wants. Think about what will motivate him to settle. You should be able to guess his objective even if he has not yet verbalized it.

You can be hard-nosed about the negotiation if you have inside knowledge about your spouse's weaknesses. If, for instance, you are certain that your spouse has a very real fear of going to court and having to testify about the marital relationship and what went wrong, you can insist on a better settlement to keep it out of court. A husband who has physically abused his wife may not want testimony about that abuse put in the public record. A wife who was involved in numerous adulterous relationships may likewise want that information kept quiet—and so may her boyfriends.

## Throw Your Spouse a Bone

You may have a very strong case, particularly if you have followed the advice in this book thus far, but even a very strong case can have an uncertain ending in court. The lawyer has to prove to his client that he has "won" something to justify his fee. Your spouse and her attorney will not accept a settlement that leaves them no worse off than if they went to court and lost. They have to feel that they are walking away from the settlement with something. Otherwise, they may decide to "take their chances in court." If you are willing to give up nothing, then your spouse has nothing to lose at trial and everything to gain. You, however, at the very least, have to contend with the emotional trauma and financial cost of a trial.

Marilyn and Tom were both suing for custody of their daughter Jennifer. I was quite certain that with the witnesses and evidence we had gathered, I could get Marilyn custody, but we were trying to negotiate a settlement to save the expense of trial. Although we had made several offers, Tom continued to stick to his demand for full custody. Finally, I brought Marilyn into my office to discuss the situation.

"What is it that your husband really wants?" I asked.

"He says he wants custody," she answered, looking at me quizzically. Hadn't I figured that much out, she must have been thinking.

"No, I mean, putting the legalities aside, does he really want Jennifer living with him and not with you?"

"I am not sure," she said "I think he is afraid he will be cut out of her life."

"Did he say that?"

"Not in so many words, but the last time we argued about it he kept saying, 'You aren't going to take my daughter away from me,' stuff like that."

I leaned forward and looked her in the eyes. "How would you feel about giving him joint custody?" I asked.

"Now wait a minute," she began. Her eyes had widened. I held up my hand to continue.

"What I mean is, give him partial custody in name only. We can propose that both of you have legal custody but that Jennifer live with you. We will set up the same visitation arrangement we offered him before. In fact, our entire proposal will be just like last time except it will now say joint custody."

"And Jennifer will continue living with me?"

"Yes. 'Joint custody' is just a legal term meaning that the two of you will have to share in any decision making for her, like her education, religion, when she dates, when she drives a car, those kinds of things."

"I would expect him to be involved in those decisions anyway," she said, relaxing, "if he would stop being such a jerk, that is."

So we made the offer. He accepted it and the divorce trial was avoided.

Marilyn and Tom both got exactly what they wanted. Tom got no more than what we had offered him before, except now he could say that he too had custody. It was a moral victory for him that did not cost my client anything. We let him walk away with something instead of making it all or nothing.

## The Red Herring

Early in the negotiations it is common to take a bargaining position that includes demanding something that you really do not care about anyway, something your spouse considers important and would judge it a victory to get or deny you. This can be anything from alimony to restrictions on visitation or, most commonly, some specific item of property. Your first settlement offer may include several of these red herrings. You can give them up one by one in subsequent offers until you settle. It is rare that we settle a case for the absolute bottom line. Usually, the client ends up with a red herring or two that did not get bargained away, little bonuses for being a good negotiator.

Kari's case is a good example. Children were not an issue since the two kids were both grown and had moved away from home. Kari and Mike had been married for twenty-six years and had managed their money carefully but were by no means wealthy. They were a fairly typical middle-class couple with five years left on their mortgage, two cars, modest savings, a few stocks, and the normal furniture and recreational items. Mike was an engineer and was looking forward to retiring in ten years. Kari was a few years younger and had worked as a licensed practical nurse off and on during the marriage. She was unemployed when Mike filed for divorce.

We determined that what Kari really wanted was half the total value of the property and temporary alimony until she found a job. She said that although she would like to get the house, it was really bigger than she needed now that the children were gone. In our first offer to settle, we asked for permanent alimony, the house, and three-quarters of the other property. In particular, we demanded that Mike's hunting cabin be sold and the proceeds divided.

Kari knew Mike dearly loved the hunting property, which he and his friends used for their annual two-week outing each autumn. The place was not worth much more than the cost of a good used car, but it had great nonmonetary value to Mike. He wanted the cabin, did not want to pay permanent alimony; his counteroffers included ever more generous offers of the total property.

Just before the trial date, we made our "final" offer. We would accept temporary alimony for two years, divide the other things fifty-fifty; she would keep the house but he would get one-fourth the equity in five years. In Mike's counteroffer he basically agreed to our proposal except he wanted the cabin and would, in return, pay her attorney fees. We quickly agreed.

Mike and his lawyer were happy since they felt that they had defeated her claim for permanent alimony and he got the cabin. Kari was thrilled to get the house, temporary alimony, and my fees paid. She got at least as much as she would have received in trial and more than her bottom line. An expensive and grueling trial was avoided and both parties remained on speaking terms.

## Knowing the Judge

This goes back to picking a lawyer who is familiar with the local court system and has practiced divorce law extensively in front of the judge who will hear your case. He can make a fairly accurate prediction as to what the judge would decide if the case goes to trial. Consequently, in negotiating you can offer to give up something that the judge would likely give your spouse anyway. The gesture makes you look very generous and open to settlement. It is similar to the red herring, except this may be something you do care about but have little or no hope of winning from that particular judge.

Finding common ground, those areas in which you and your opponent do agree, and getting them settled first is a common negotiating technique but one I do not like in divorce. True, it narrows the issues for settlement, but I have found that if you hold the entire package open, you are more likely to end up with what you really want. Otherwise, you may bargain away everything except what you really want and end up going to trial over that one issue with perhaps only a fifty-fifty chance of getting it from the judge. Some states hold what are called "bifurcated trials," in which the issues are separated. For example, the parties may have agreed on the property issues but go to trial over custody. In my mind, some of your bargaining leverage is taken away if the issue you go to trial over is of primary importance to you. Keep all the options open. Either settle everything or take all of it to trial.

If your spouse is reluctant to settle, you can gradually narrow the issues by negotiating "mini-settlements." Instead of proposing one big settlement package, do it in installments. First the house, then the car, then the MasterCard bill, then the pension plan, and so on. You can make what you really want one of the first items to be settled; then everything you get from that point on is a bonus.

Negotiating in a divorce case normally is not done face-to-face. I have tried this method occasionally with only limited success. Too often, the couple is unable to sit across from one another at a table and rationally discuss settlement. The emotional climate is so intense that negotiations go nowhere. They tell me that they feel pressured in these situations and are rarely both satisfied with any agreement that is reached.

In my experience, written offers are the most effective method of settling a divorce case. I spell out the specific terms of each section of the divorce as I would like it entered by the judge. If the other side agrees, they sign it and send it back. Sometimes they actually agree to our first offer; most often, the other side makes a written counteroffer, which I then review with my client. Eventually, we can reach a meeting of the minds. It is a give-and-take method used while waiting for a trial date. If we are unable to agree, then there is always the trial and we have not delayed the proceedings at all.

If your spouse has a job that is political in nature or involves dealing with the conservative attitudes of his superiors and co-workers, he may likewise prefer a settlement even if he has to give you more than the court likely would. Know your enemy. You can use his fear of going to court to your advantage. Remember the section in chapter 5 about extortion? It may well be that laying out your spouse's financial dealings to the judge would get him in a lot of hot water with the tax people or prosecutors. He would probably prefer to settle on your terms.

## Mediation

Mediation is being used more often these days. The court may order that the attorneys present their cases to a mediator or mediation panel. The mediator hears the evidence on both sides, including transcripts of the expected testimony of all the witnesses and all documentary evidence. Issues of law are briefed by the attorneys and presented to the mediator. After reviewing everything, the mediator will make a recommendation that is sometimes filed with the court, containing his proposed disposition of all issues of the case. The parties can then choose whether to accept the findings of the mediator. Sometimes there are even penalties for not accepting the mediator's recommendation if you insist on a trial and do no better than you would have done by accepting the recommendation. If your case is strong, mediation is a great idea. It can improve your bargaining position and be a shortcut to a good settlement.

Suppose you "win" the mediation and your spouse still refuses to settle? In that case, you can sometimes avoid a trial by accepting less than what the mediator recommended so long as the difference is less than the cost of taking the case to court. Your spouse and his attorney will feel like they have won something, while you walk away with most of the marbles.

Private mediation services are now becoming more common. Depending upon the arrangement you make and the law in your state, the private mediator, paid for by the divorcing couple, can make a binding settlement of most issues. The legal basis would be the contractual agreement both sides made with the mediation service before the case was heard. Even a nonbinding private mediation recommendation can make a recalcitrant spouse see the light and give up unrealistic bargaining positions.

Going to trial is definitely the last resort. Do everything you can to settle the case so long as you get what you really have to have. Going through a divorce trial is not a pleasant experience for you, your spouse, or your children.

# CHAPTER TEN

# DOING BATTLE: THE TRIAL

L et's assume that every attempt you have made to settle has failed. Although you have avoided trial like the plague, your spouse is intractable and refuses to make any reasonable deals. Divorce court is looming ahead. Fear not. If you go into this prepared, you will have a great advantage over your opponent.

First, it is important to understand the role of the judge and how the court works. Then, you can make a battle plan based upon the workings of the system. Judges really do want to do the right thing. They try very hard to be fair and each of them sees himself as Solomon, trying the cases with divinely inspired judgment.

Your job is to give the judge reasons to decide in your favor.

## Muster the Troops

After listening to all the witnesses from both sides, analyzing the documents, and hearing the arguments of the lawyers, the judge is supposed to make a series of decisions supported by all the evidence. You have to give the judge a separate logical reason to support each of the decisions you want him to make. Give him something to hang his hat on. You need more than just your own statements as to what is fair. He will listen to your testimony, but you can make his job ever so much easier by giving him other specific evidence to support the difficult decisions he must make. Let's look at an example of an actual divorce trial to illustrate my point.

Harry and Karen had been married for sixteen years and had two children, ages twelve and fourteen. Custody and property division were the main things at stake. Harry was a good father, as Karen herself admitted. He spent a lot of time with the two children even after he moved into an apartment when Karen filed for divorce. He turned down overtime on his job as a bricklayer to spend more time with them. Harry did not want the divorce, but once Karen filed, he was determined not to give up custody and become a "visiting father." He was sure that since Karen started the divorce, and in fact had been unfaithful during the marriage, the judge would give him custody. He hired a lawyer reluctantly, planning originally to present his own case to the judge. After all, fair is fair and facts are facts, right?

Karen had carefully prepared her case. During the trial she brought in the children's school counselors and teachers who testified that it was Karen who always came to the teacher conferences. They had never even seen Harry before. A child psychologist testified that she had interviewed both children and in her expert opinion their well-being would best be served by keeping them with their mother. Karen herself had been seen by a psychologist, who said she was a stable, responsible person well able to care for the kids. Neighbors testified that Karen was a very attentive mother, always keeping track of the children's whereabouts. Mrs. Potts, who lived next door, explained that she had watched the children grow up in the neighborhood and could not imagine them living anywhere else. Even the minister came into court and testified about Karen's activities with the church youth group. Karen's accountant testified about the value of the marital assets, and her vocational rehabilitation counselor discussed Karen's ability to earn an income.

Harry's attorney did his best to cross-examine the witnesses and minimize the impact of their testimony. He even got Karen to admit on the witness stand that Harry was a good father and had a wonderful relationship with the children. Finally, Harry took the stand and explained his devotion to the children and his plans for taking care of them should he get custody. He had no witnesses to support him, but said he was sure the kids would be happy with him, and anyway, the divorce was not his fault.

Karen made the judge's decision very easy. Before him he had two good parents. Both would be suitable for custody and the children would be happy with either one. (The children, in fact, had expressed no preference when they talked to the judge in his office.) Without much ado he awarded custody to Karen, because she gave him a lot of reasons to do so. He could easily justify his decision by pointing to the testimony of the minister, teachers, neighbors, and psychologists.

Karen also got the house, because the judge said it would disrupt the children's lives too much to ask them to move out of the place where they had grown up. Harry got visitation, a lien on the house for his property interest in it, and a support order.

Karen got everything she really wanted and then some.

The point is, in a divorce trial, just as in a battle, the more firepower you bring to bear, the greater your likelihood of victory. Make it easy for the judge to dispense justice in your favor.

## Pick the Right Battlefield

It is sometimes possible to arrange where you will get divorced to maximize your chances of victory. For example, if receiving alimony is your primary objective, do not file for divorce in Texas. By statute, the judge cannot give it to you. Reestablish residency elsewhere and file the divorce there. If your goal is just to get a divorce and your spouse plans on fighting it, move to a state with a pure no-fault divorce law and a short waiting period. Then you do not have to worry whether or not he will "give" you a divorce. Each state has specific laws that may act for or against your objectives.

If children are involved, moving to another state can present a problem. There is a law called the Uniform Child Custody Jurisdiction Act (UCCJA), an example of which is given in appendix E. The act states that once a custody case has been started in one jurisdiction, another case may not be started in a new jurisdiction; it also sets out rules to determine which of two competing states is the proper one to decide custody issues.

If you move away with the children and sue for custody after establishing legal residency, you may prevent your spouse from having the case heard where she lives. You have thus put her at a great disadvantage since she will have to defend the case via long distance. Her costs and the difficulty in fighting you will increase.

But be careful. If your spouse can prove that you did not establish a legal residence in the new state and that your intention was merely to take advantage of the different divorce laws existing there, the divorce can be dismissed or transferred back to your original jurisdiction. Keep in mind that if you do not take the children, you cannot start a custody case in the new state. The children have no significant connection to the new state and the court does not have authority over them. And if a case has already been started, you cannot go to another jurisdiction and start a new one if you do not like the way things are going.

If you want the new residency to stick, do the things that indicate you really are serious about changing your residence. Get a driver's license in the new state. Register to vote. Rent an apartment. Get a job. After everything is over, you are free to move anywhere you like—even back from where you came. This is America.

What if it really isn't feasible to move to another state just to get divorced? If you are able to move within the state, you may still be able to gain an advantage by having your divorce heard in another county.

In Michigan, where I practice law, the Wayne County courts are a mess. The court procedures are lengthy, the Friend of the Court (the agency that makes child custody and support recommendations) is overburdened, and everyone in general is overworked. If you want a fast, simple divorce, Wayne County is not where you want to be. Your attorney fees will be high just because of the amount of time it takes to deal with the bureaucracy, waiting for court hearings, and excessive paperwork.

However, if you go right next door to Washtenaw County, it is as if you have gone to another world. The procedures are simple and straightforward, the clerks are helpful, and the cases proceed quickly.

Maybe you have seen the advertisements for "same day" divorces in the Dominican Republic or Mexico. Beware! You may find that you have paid for a very expensive quick divorce, parts of which are enforceable and valid only in the country in which it was issued. Further, the courts in your home state may not recognize the authority of a foreign country to decide issues relating to child custody, alimony, or real estate located in your home state. You would have to start a whole new case back at home to decide these issues and to have a forum in which to enforce them.

It is possible then to pick a forum that will be most likely to advance your strategy. Do you want to make it difficult and expensive for your spouse as an inducement to settle? If so, then file in an overburdend system like Wayne County. Note that every state has its own residency requirements and each court system has its own peculiarities. In Alaska, for instance, you can file for divorce the day you get there. You must talk to an attorney before you file to find out about the court systems in that area.

## Strike the First Blow

Choice of forum, as I have just explained, is a good reason to file first. You pick the battlefield. Even if there are no children, you cannot have two divorce cases going on at the same time. The first one started is the one that is litigated. The other must be dismissed.

Another very good reason to act first is that you have the opportunity to get temporary court orders favoring you. Upon the filing of the case, the plaintiff can have the judge enter orders for such things as temporary custody, child support, visitation, temporary alimony, and injunctions. In most cases these orders cannot be set aside without a formal hearing in front of the judge. There is even some case law that says that the person seeking to set aside a temporary order has to show good cause for the change. This means that if all things are equal on each side, the first one to court gets the advantage.

## Defend Yourself

"I got taken to the cleaners."

People often come to me and lament the poor treatment they received from a divorce. Most of the time the reason the hapless defendants were treated so poorly is because they did not truly defend themselves.

*If you are served divorce papers, see a lawyer immediately!*

I have heard a local judge say the following words just before granting a divorce plaintiff's request for all the property, custody, child support, and alimony:

"If the defendant cared, he would be here, so it must be alright with him. Motion granted."

Put yourself in the judge's chair. He has proof that the defendant has been served with a summons and a complaint, knows about the divorce and the court hearing, yet does not show up. The only person the judge hears from is the plaintiff. Naturally, he does what she wants. It is the same situation that would exist if your team fails to show up for the big game. The other side wins by default.

Don't listen to the advice of your spouse that you don't need a lawyer because this is "no-fault." If you do not have a lawyer, it is *your fault* if you get less than you deserve.

## Grounds for Divorce

The fact is that in most states fault has no statutory bearing on whether or not the divorce will be granted. Whether it is called "irreconcilable differences" or "a breakdown in the marriage relationship to the extent that the objects of matrimony have been destroyed and the marriage can no longer be preserved," no-fault laws eliminate the worry of whether your spouse will "give" you a divorce. Anyone who wants one can have it, and, therefore, there really are no grounds needed for divorce. The disputes in courts nowadays are not over the divorce itself, but, instead, are over the issues of children, money, and property. However, fault is still very important. The old "grounds for divorce" of cruelty, desertion, alcoholism, and adultery may not be on the statute books anymore in a lot of states, but they sure can make a difference to a judge in decision making. Remember what I said about giving the judge something to hang his hat on? If he hears that you are recovering from alcohol or drug addiction, he will use that information against you in deciding your case.

The lesson here? If you have something on your spouse, you can use it in trial—or threaten to. Sometimes, just the fear of having the ugly details revealed will facilitate a last-minute settlement. Nearly anything is relevant in a divorce trial since the character of the parties is a matter at issue, particularly in custody cases. In fact, by statute, even in some no-fault states, fault can be looked at to decide custody, alimony, and property issues.

If you are the one who was at fault, remember that the details will likely be spread out in court for everyone to hear. Your best bet is to let your spouse think you are looking forward to going to court and do not care about revealing the details—then, work very hard for a settlement.

Although it is becoming less necessary to prove fault in order to get a divorce (the majority of states now have some form of "no-fault" divorce), there are still places where you must prove that your spouse is responsible for the breakdown of the marriage to qualify for a divorce. The most common grounds listed in the statutes are cruelty, desertion, alcoholism, adultery, nonsupport, and conviction of a felony. If you can prove he was guilty of any of these, then you qualify for a divorce.

Talk to a local attorney to discover the requirements for divorce in your state. Sometimes the grounds are established by what we lawyers call a "legal fiction," or in layman's terms, a lie. I recall one jurisdiction that, before it changed to no-fault, required a "correspondent" to testify as to the grounds for divorce. This was a third person who could corroborate the statements in the divorce complaint that the grounds for divorce did indeed exist.

One major law firm specializing in divorce always seemed to name the same person as the correspondent, a person who claimed to have been involved in an adulterous relationship with the plaintiff. In fact, when someone researched the cases, it was found that this woman had claimed to have been involved in adulterous relationships with thousands of the

firm's divorce clients. As it turned out, she was one of the
legal secretaries in the firm and had never had a relationship
with anyone but her own husband. It was a lie used to get
around the stringent requirements that existed to qualify for a
divorce. Getting grounds is usually not a problem.

## Reinforcements

When things are going very badly, there is sometimes help
available.

I once had a client, Clara, who was as bad as one could
get. She was addicted to Valium in addition to being a severe
alcoholic. She had prescriptions from eight different doctors
for her drugs. Her temper was volatile, she used filthy language,
and had a succession of boyfriends during the marriage. She
was fighting for custody of her two small children, a boy and
girl, six and eight years old.

Fortunately for Clara, if not for her kids, the husband was
not much better. He was also an alcoholic, and involved with
numerous women. He worked occasionally, but usually only
long enough to qualify for unemployment compensation.

If I had been the judge, I would not have wanted to give
custody to either of these parents—so I explored other options.
Clara told me her mother lived in town and would be willing to
accept custody. I developed a proposal for the judge to place the
children with the maternal grandmother, but then something
fortuitous happened: Clara's mother hired her own lawyer.

Now we had three separate petitions for custody with
three lawyers. Clara had no problem with her mother getting
custody, so, in essence, when we went to trial it was two
against one. The judge now had a reasonable alternative and
gave the grandmother custody after hearing how bad the parents were. Clara later moved in with her mother and wound
up with custody—if not in law, then in fact. The children were
better off and so, I think, was Clara.

Grandparents can petition for custody or visitation on
their own with their own lawyer if there is an ongoing custody dispute. This right can be an added bonus to you if your
own case is weak. You can utilize the rights of your parents to
get further visitation time with your children.

Reinforcements can also take the form of expert witnesses. Remember the story of Harry and Karen at the beginning of the chapter? Get more troops on your side. Judges like specialists. A child psychologist testifying that the children are better off with you will carry more weight than you telling the judge the same thing. A certified public accountant (CPA) testifying as to the value of your spouse's professional practice will convince the judge of its value more than simply showing the tax returns (but put the tax returns into evidence, too). The CPA can also value specific assets and testify as to the tax consequences of alimony or specific distributions of property.

A physician testifying about your poor physical condition or an employment counselor testifying about the poor job market for people with your skills will bolster your claim for alimony.

## Ammunition

The best ammunition you can have is your written records. Judges love written records and much prefer them to recollections. If you have kept a diary of your marriage, detailing all the good things you have done and all the bad things your spouse has done, then you have a full ammunition clip.

My client Dierdre showed up in court with six calendars, one for each year since the children had entered school. She had written down every time she took them to Girl Scouts, piano lessons, parent-teacher conferences, music programs, doctor appointments, and dental visits. Her husband also claimed to have taken the kids, but Dierdre denied it. Dierdre had evidence. Her husband just had his recollections. Dierdre won. I am not saying that keeping track of things like Dierdre did will cinch your case. You can still lose, but you increase your odds by having more ammunition on your side.

Similar records can be kept on marital fault. How many times did she come home drunk? Did he take the kids to a bar instead of to the park? When? If your spouse has assaulted you, write down the details and the dates. Take Polaroids of the bruises and write the dates on the back. Get documentary proof of drunk driving and other criminal convictions or arrests. Write down the times he drove drunk but was not caught. A written record always carries weight with the judge.

## Your Code of Conduct

Your civilized demeanor in court should go without saying. But let me say a few words on the subject anyway.

- DO NOT lose your temper on the witness stand.
- DO NOT interrupt the testimony of your spouse or any other witness even when you know they are lying.
- DO NOT answer more than you are asked. Volunteering information usually only hurts you.
- DO dress conservatively and appropriately. Dress as if you were going to church.
- DO practice your testimony with your attorney before going into court. Have a "trial run" so that you will know what to expect. Your attorney should also give you a practice cross-examination so that you will know what the other side will ask you.

Be polite and act just like the kind of person who deserves to get what he or she really wants. If you are properly prepared, have all the right witnesses and physical evidence, and are in the appropriate courtroom, your chances of achieving your objectives are terrific.

# CHAPTER ELEVEN

# COUNTERATTACK

So, you went to trial and lost. Or you did not get everything that you really wanted. Don't worry. You are not defeated yet.

## Appeal

If your lawyer did his job properly, there are issues to appeal. The law says that questions of law may be appealed, but unless the judge made a decision against the great weight of the evidence or clearly abused his discretion, questions of judgment are not appealable. Leave the technicalities to your lawyer. What you need to know is that appeals are very expensive and just the threat of going ahead with an appeal can sometimes get you a more generous settlement than what the judge gave you. I have heard it called extortion, but there is nothing improper about taking full advantage of all the legal avenues available; cumbersome, time consuming, and expensive though they may be.

Appealing is the legal procedure in which another higher court reviews the decision made by the trial judge to see if she made any mistakes of law. You may win an appeal in a custody case if, for instance, your judge did not consider the custody factors in coming to her decision. Perhaps she refused to let you admit the testimony of your child's psychologist or did not admit any evidence of the child's preference. These are examples of "reversible errors" and can be the basis of a successful appeal.

The problem with appeals in divorce cases is that usually you do not win the case just because you win the appeal. Most of the time the appeals court sends the case back to the trial judge with instructions to correct the error; then the case must be retried. The appeal will likely cost at least as much as the divorce itself had up to that point and then you must start again with the trial and possibly another appeal. It is very expensive, which is why it is a good bargaining chip.

You don't want to appeal? Well, there are still things that can be done.

## Custody

The custody case is never over. It is sad but true that the court retains continuing jurisdiction over the divorce case until the children all reach the age of majority. Consequently, a petition for change of custody can be filed any time after the divorce is finalized. Statutes and case law in different states will set out the basis for such a petition. Generally, they all allow it if there has been a "material change in circumstances" and it is "in the best interests of the children." This kind of language leaves a lot of room for interpretation and so it is fairly easy to come up with reasons why a change of custody is necessary.

My client Leonard was awarded custody of his daughter Tabitha after a long and bitter divorce trial. Her mother Rose was determined not to give up. Only three weeks after the divorce was finalized Rose filed a petition to change custody, alleging that Leonard was not providing sufficient supervision for Tabitha and that since she had now remarried, she was able to provide a more stable home environment for the child. There was a hearing before the judge on Rose's petition. The judge referred the whole matter to the Friend of the Court Referee, who held a complete evidentiary hearing, listening to witnesses and my arguments and those of Rose's attorney, and then the Referee's decision was reviewed by the judge in yet another hearing. Rose lost again.

A year later, Rose filed another petition, citing a whole list of new reasons for the requested change. The process was the same. We filed an answer, defended in all the hearings, and won again.

Rose continued to file petitions, sometimes only weeks after losing the previous one. This went on for several years. I asked the judge to institute sanctions for frivolous litigation, but he refused, saying she had every right to ask for a change of custody so long as she had good reasons. Eventually, Tabitha took matters into her own hands, telling her mother emphatically that she wanted to stay with her father. Tabitha was by then fifteen. Rose gave up.

In other circumstances, Rose may well have won. Had Leonard not been willing to continue the fight, he may well have lost custody. She was hoping to win just by wearing him down.

## Support

Support is another area where the divorce judgment can be changed. If there is a change of circumstances, support can sometimes be increased or decreased depending upon the provisions of your state's laws. Say your ex gets a new job with higher pay. If you have custody, you can ask for more support; if you do not have custody, you can ask that you pay less support. Any time there is a significant change in income levels for either parent, a change in support levels may be necessary.

More and more often, courts rely upon charts to determine support levels. The charts generally factor together the incomes of both parents and the number of children to arrive at a support amount. Request one of the charts from your lawyer, or if they are available online, download one from your computer. You can then keep track of what the courts would give you and file for an increase or decrease when it looks worthwhile.

Just the passage of time may justify an increase in support. Most divorce judgments do not set child support at a specific percentage of income, but rather as a simple dollar amount. After several years, inflation will have eroded the support amount such that it is worth less in buying power than it was originally. Ask for an increase every two years. Sometimes you do not need a lawyer at all to increase or decrease support levels. The court often has an agency that will do this for you.

All the court can do is say no, so do not be afraid to ask for the increase. Jenny got her divorce when her three children were ages four, six, and nine. The support order was for $150 each week, based on the father's income at the time of the divorce. Jenny struggled, went to school, got a job, bought a house, and continued to collect the same support amount until the oldest was eighteen years old. She had needed an increase in her support payments for years but was afraid her ex-husband would be angry and drag her through court again. I explained that the process was not the same as when she had gotten the original divorce, but she was intimidated by him and would not take any steps to ask for an increase.

Finally, her ex-husband petitioned the court for a decrease, saying that now that the oldest was of legal age he should only have to pay for two children. That spurred Jenny to action. She countered with a request for an increase, based on his increased income and won! Now she is getting $200 in support payments a week for two children. She would have gotten an increase years before had she asked. Do not be afraid to ask.

## Enforcement of Judgments

Even when the judge says you win, what do you do if your ex-spouse refuses to comply? The divorce judgment is, after all, just a piece of paper, right? Wrong. There are plenty of things you can do to enforce the terms of your divorce.

### *Property*

If your ex-husband refuses to turn over property to you that was properly awarded in the judgment, he can be brought back to court on an "order to show cause." Essentially, the judge will ask him why he should not be held in contempt of court and be jailed for refusing to obey the judgment. He better have some pretty good reasons. If you are entitled to specific money payments, you can sometimes use garnishment to attach your former spouse's wages or bank accounts to collect. For instance, suppose you were supposed to receive $5,000 within six months after the divorce as payment for your share of your ex-husband's Corvette. If he refuses to pay, you can have the money deducted from his bank accounts or taken in installments from his paycheck. You could also "execute" on his personal property (have his Corvette seized and sold) or file a lien against his real estate, which can then be foreclosed. Check your local laws to see which of these remedies are available. Some divorce lawyers are not aware that money obligations for property in a divorce are collectible like any other money judgments.

### Alimony and Child Support

*There is a debtor's prison.* The judge can put a support payer in jail for refusing to pay child support or alimony. Nowadays, most judgments have the support deducted directly from the payer's paycheck so there is no problem with collection. But, people change jobs, leave the state, or become unemployed. Isn't it tough to get support then? Not necessarily.

All fifty states now enforce each other's support orders. There is a federal law that allows the tracking of social security numbers to locate support payers. They can run but they cannot hide. Even those who leave the country are not totally out of the woods. The support accrues and is enforceable against the property of the debtor. His tax refunds are intercepted. If you are persistent, you can get your money. Refer to appendix C for the Uniform Interstate Family Support Act, a new federal law mandated for all the states that makes interstate collection of child support much easier.

## Custody Help Outside the Courts

If you believe the other parent has an unsuitable environment in which she is keeping the children, it is possible to get help from the state. Most states have agencies responsible for child welfare and will investigate complaints made about children being kept in unwholesome environments. They often will remove the children from the custodial parent and place them in foster care or with the other parent if the living situation is bad enough.

I have used this tactic myself when the situation merited it. My client calls the child protective service agency, which then makes an unannounced inspection of the custodial parent's home. The investigator is an excellent witness in our petition to change custody. Note also that the name of the person making the initial complaint is usually kept confidential.

## Revenge

If you have lost and exhausted all available legal remedies, I honestly think it is better to lick your wounds and go on with your life. Unfortunately, not everyone is able to do that. With that in mind, it is a good idea to protect yourself from the possible retaliation of your former spouse.

Cancel your credit cards and get new ones issued (assuming you did not do it before you filed for divorce, as I suggested). One of my clients learned his lesson when his ex-wife ran up thousands of dollars in charges on his credit cards after the divorce was over. He had not bothered to notify them of the divorce and did not know his wife still had her cards. Change the locks on the marital home if you won it in the divorce. It is surprising how often there are "burglaries" after the divorce trial.

If your former spouse knows about illegal or immoral activities in which you have been involved and would rather keep quiet, there may not be much you can do but hope. Getting rid of the evidence is about all I can suggest. But if your ex was the one behaving badly, be careful about telling on him. Turning in your ex can sometimes backfire.

One of my clients came to me after the divorce seeking help with a tax fraud case. It seems she and her former husband were being charged with tax evasion for underreporting their income during the marriage. She explained that he had been doing side work as a mechanic in the family garage and had never reported any of the cash transactions. After the divorce she reported him to the IRS. The IRS filed charges against both of them since they had always filed joint returns. Since I do not do criminal or tax work, I referred her to another attorney, but the story illustrates the dangers of seeking revenge.

# CHAPTER TWELVE

# CLOSING ARGUMENTS

We have covered the divorce war from planning the beginning skirmish to living with victory or defeat. The important thing to do now is get some perspective.

The real danger of the entire divorce proceeding is getting so wrapped up emotionally in battling your spouse that you lose sight of your ultimate goal. Keep the overall game plan in mind throughout the proceedings. Your goal should always be motivating your actions. Keep the hostility directed elsewhere. Seek counseling if necessary to deal with the emotional turmoil of the separation process, but do not allow those emotions to color your divorce planning.

Here is a summary of what you should do.

1. **Plan for divorce before it happens.**
   If possible, even before you get married. Get a premarital agreement in writing. During the marriage, keep a calendar or diary detailing your involvement with the children. Keep informed of all your spouse's financial dealings. Arrange the ownership of property to your advantage.

2. **Define your objective.**
   If a divorce is imminent, what is your ideal, but realistically obtainable, end result? Keep this objec-

tive to yourself, but keep it foremost in your mind throughout the proceedings.

**3. Get a separation agreement.**

You can strengthen your case substantially and will find it easier to get a settlement before any divorce is filed while your spouse may still be holding onto some thread of hope for a reconciliation.

**4. Make a custody plan.**

Have your evidence and witnesses available to you so that you have more provable "points" than your spouse.

**5. Make a property plan.**

Time the divorce properly if either of you is still in school or about to come into money. Stay in the marital home if you want to keep it, and stay with the children if you want to keep them. Most of all, stay informed.

**6. Pick a divorce expert for your lawyer.**

Your brother-in-law might be a terrific guy and a terrific probate lawyer, but don't let him handle your divorce.

**7. Never take legal advice from your spouse.**

Even if he is not intentionally lying to you, he might be just plain wrong.

**8. Negotiate—intelligently and strenuously—rather than go to trial.**

Get the case settled for financial and peace-of-mind reasons. Use every available tactic to get a settlement. Don't give up your ultimate objective. Demand something important to your spouse so that you can give it up later to get what you really want.

**9. Give the judge something to hang his hat on.**

Use expert witnesses. Put yourself in his place. Give him lots of reasons why he should give you what you want.

10. **Throw your spouse a bone.**
He and his attorney have to leave with something or they will have nothing to lose by going to trial. Just make sure the something that you give them is not what you really want.

11. **Do not use the children as weapons.**
They are not the ones getting a divorce. No matter how bad your spouse is, the children still love him or her and deserve to have that parent-child relationship.

12. **Be certain that a divorce is what you really want.**
You may be able to achieve your objective in some less drastic manner. Remember the dangers of divorce.

Next to the death of a child, parent, or spouse, divorce is the most devastating and traumatic event in a person's life. It will unalterably change everyone involved and will have a major impact on the finances of both the husband and the wife. It is vitally important that you handle such an important life event in the most intelligent and thought-out manner possible. I have used the war analogy in the preceding pages because you must force yourself to view the adversarial situation with as much objectivity as possible if you hope to achieve a result that will benefit you the most.

After you are divorced, be sure to update your will and estate plan. A divorce invalidates what you had done previously. Also be sure to name new beneficiaries on your insurance policies and IRAs. Attorneys sometimes forget to tell their clients these things. If you should decide to remarry, consider a prenuptial agreement before you take the plunge, particularly if you have children, so that their interests are protected.

I can go on for hundreds of more pages telling you about the intricacies of the legal process and specific statutes that may apply to your case, but that is why you hire a lawyer. What you have just read is intended to keep you on the track of getting a final divorce result that satisfies your basic needs, helps you identify and get what you really want, and keeps your spouse from taking advantage of you.

Good luck!

# FAMILY LAW
# INTERNET RESOURCES

The Internet has an incredible amount of information on nearly every subject, including divorce and family law. Finding the best sources of information is difficult without some starting points and that is what I am going to provide here.

You can also use the Internet as a sort of therapy by utilizing some of the divorce bulletin boards and chat rooms to correspond with others similarly situated. On the bulletin boards you can pose questions or state problems and get feedback. Keep in mind that the advice you get is not necessarily good advice. It is free and you get what you pay for. The value in participating in these forums is twofold. First, you get to vent your feelings. That is good in itself since you are relatively anonymous on the Net and do not need to hold anything back. Second, you see that there are lots of other fellow sufferers out there—some with much worse situations than yours.

The information available breaks down into four basic areas. Referrals to agencies, attorneys, and firms that can assist you in the divorce process; articles addressing various divorce and parent-child issues; governmental information such as statutes, court procedures, court decisions, and information on government agencies; and Web sites of divorce lawyers, mediators, financial planners, booksellers, and others who profit from the divorce business.

There are literally tens of thousands of sites related to divorce. I list a few of the better ones of which I am aware at the time we go to press. Remember, though, that the Web is ever changing. I may not have listed some good sources, and new sources will no doubt come into existence on a daily basis from now on. Most sites have links that, if followed, will connect you with other sites that have links that will connect you ad infinitum to all the other links eventually. The following are Web sites with which to begin. I list these along with their links in my newly created Web site at **www.windivorce.com.**

### www.divorcenet.com

This very well designed Web site for the *Family Law Advisor* has as its best feature a variety of very good articles from the newsletter on a wide range of topics. Put out by the law office of Sharon T. Sooho in Newton, Massachusetts, it has a well-used bulletin board with divorce litigants spilling their problems and divorce survivors telling war stories. The links are good for the most part, but the professional referrals are only to those attorneys and others who pay for the listing service, so you have no assurance that the referral is to someone skilled or experienced in your particular situation.

The Web site does have a state-by-state resource center listing that might prove useful. The visitor counter showed 17,358,549 hits for 1997, so someone is using it.

### www.divorceinfo.com

Attorney Lee Borden of Birmingham, Alabama, has created this extremely comprehensive site that is easy to read. He claims it is equivalent to a seven hundred–page book. Its down-home chatty style is sometimes entertaining and it has articles and information on nearly every aspect of divorce. However, it has very few links to other sites. Referral attorneys do not pay a fee and have to promise Borden that they get at least 75 percent of their income from doing divorce-related work. This requirement must be his form of quality control. He attempts to sell a set of divorce information kits and videos, but is not pushy about it. I do recommend the site because of the vast coverage of its articles. It reads at times like Borden's home page, with one page about his wife, one about his church, and another about his "worthless yellow lab" complete with picture.

### www.divorcecentral.com

An excellent site for links and resources to many divorce-related sites on the Web. There are chat rooms and bulletin boards so that you can "get it off your chest" and get support from others. One unique feature is a personals page where I suppose you can match up with some other distraught divorce litigant. When I viewed it, there were only a half-dozen or so personal ads listed and only one was a woman. As I said, this is a good site for links.

**www.divorcesource.com and www.divorcesupport.com**

These seem to be the same site and it is hard to tell when you are in one and not the other since they are designed the same way. These sites are heavily promoted, with ads throughout the Web linking to them. There are chat rooms, links to other sites, and a divorce dictionary. There are links to divorce-related books for sale online with reviews provided. The site is very commercial and not a comprehensive listing of what is available. The state-by-state and Canadian resources are links to members who pay a fee so the referral is no indication of quality and they make no such representation. There are many articles supplied by the resource links on divorce-related issues such as money, the legal process, and psychological aspects. It gets heavy use with almost 300,000 visits its first year. You can e-mail your specific questions and get an answer from "Ask the Divorced Guy" and "Ask the Divorced Woman." Remember to rely on the advice of your lawyer, not the invisible face on the Net.

**www.divorce-online.com**

When I looked at this site, there were limited referrals, primarily in Michigan. Referral attorneys, financial, psychological, and real estate people have to pay a monthly fee to participate, so I can't recommend any of these one way or the other. It has a bulletin board called "Your Two Cents," which can be interesting, but when I looked at it, all the comments were at least nine months old. (What's up with that? There's a suggestion box that I am tempted to use.) There are good articles on some subjects.

**www.divorcelawinfo.com**

This is a Maryland company selling do-it-yourself divorce kits. If you insist against all good sense on going that way, I will give you a few others to compare prices:

- **www.iimagers.com/divorce2.html:** This is the site of the Divorce Institute that will prepare your divorce papers for you for a fee and send them online for you to file.

- **www.divorcewizards.com:** This site is also worth checking. It is a paid referral service that offers seminars and self help.

- **www.int-divorce.com:** Want a quick divorce with no hassles from your spouse or the annoying trip to court? Try this Dominican Republic by-mail divorce service run by a firm in London. All I can say is that you are divorced as far as the Dominican Republic is concerned. Just don't put a lot of faith in enforcing your decree in a U.S. court without your spouse's consent.

**http://intertain.com/store/hernew-browse/love sex and marriage-divorce.htm**

If you can type all that into your computer correctly, you will have access to an online bookstore with lots of divorce-related books you can order via the Net.

**www.divorcehelp.com**

California attorney Ed Sherman's site has referrals to mediators, attorneys, financial planners, and the like who have paid a fee to be listed. A "Short Course in Divorce" is a summary of Sherman's book. Read the short course and you may not need to spend the $14.95.

**www.divorcelawyerinfo.com**

This Web site is designed to sell *How to Find the Right Divorce Lawyer*, a book by Robin Page West, J.D.

**www.floridadivorce.com**

This Web site, by attorney Arnie B. Guskin of Fort Lauderdale, has an extremely limited discussion page that sounds like Guskin is talking to himself and suggesting he call himself for more information or to set an appointment. He does offer to answer your legal questions, but the site has little useful information or links to resources. Check it out—maybe it will change by the time you read this.

**www.supportkids.com**

A private company that will help you collect your past-due child support. Fees are charged only if it is successful. A last resort if normal channels are not successful.

**www.law.cornell.edu/**

The Legal Information Institute at Cornell Law School offers a very helpful information-filled site with many statutes, uniform laws, court rules, court decisions, and links to other sources.

I have not listed the many links to organizations that can help you. You can find these on my Web site or some of the ones above, or look in the following resource appendix for names, addresses, and telephone numbers.

## State-by-State Web Sites for Bar Associations and State Information

*Alabama*
Alabama Judicial System                    http://204.29.92.2

*Alaska*
Alaska Court System                         www.alaska.net/~akctlib/
                                            homepage.htm

*Arizona*
Arizona Judicial Index                    www.state.az.us/pages/
                                          judicial.htm

The Superior Court,                       www.sc.pima.gov
Pima County

The Self-Service Center,                  www.maricopa.gov/supcrt/
Maricopa County                           ssc/sschome.html

*Arkansas*
Arkansas Bar Association                  www.arkbar.com

Supreme Court Opinions                    www.state.ar.us/supremecourt

*California*
California Bar Association                 www.calbar.org

Judicial Branch of the                    www.courtinfo.ca.gov
State of California

Superior Courts:
    Alameda County                        www.co.alameda.ca.us/
                                          courts/superior/

    Los Angeles County                    www.co.la.ca.us/courts/
                                          superior-auc/

    Orange County                         www.oc.ca.goc.superior/

    Sacramento                            www.sna.com/courts/

*Colorado*
Colorado Bar Association                  www.usa.net/cobar/

Colorado Courts Home Page                 www.courts.state.co.us/
                                          ct-index.htm

*Connecticut*
Connecticut Bar Association               www.ctbar.org/

Judicial Information                      http://neal.ctstateu.edu:
                                          2001/statenet/judicial/
                                          index.html

*Delaware*
Delaware Court Home Page                  www.ncsc.dni.us/court/
                                          delaware/homepage.htm

*District of Columbia*
Bar Association                           www.badc.org/

*Florida*
Florida Bar Association

Florida Legal
Research Collection

*Georgia*
Georgia State Bar Association

Georgia Supreme Court

Georgia Office of Child
Support Enforcement

*Hawaii*
Hawaii State Bar Association

Hawaii Supreme Court

*Idaho*
Judicial Branch Home Page

*Illinois*
Illinois State Bar Association

State Court Opinions

*Indiana*
Indiana State Bar Association

Supreme Court

*Iowa*
Iowa Supreme Court

*Requires user name and password*
To get one:

*Kansas*
Kansas State Bar Association

Kansas Court System

www.FLABAR.org/

http://justice.courts.state.
fl.us/courts/supct/
bookmark.html

www.gabar.org/

www.state.ga.us/Courts/
Supreme/

www.2.state.ga.us/
Departments/DHR/CSE/

www.hsba.org/

www.hsba.org/Hawaii/
Court/cour.htm

www.state.id.us/judicial.html

www.illinoisbar.org/

www.state.il.us/court/
Opinions.htm

www.iquest.net/isba/

www.ai.org/judiciary/
welcome.html

http://ialaw.giant.net/
ialaw/opscdindex.html

http://ialaw.giant.net/

www.ink.org/public/cybar/

http://lark.cc.ukans.edu/
~kulawlib/kscourts.html

*Kentucky*
Kentucky State Bar Association          www.kybar.org/

Supreme Court          www.tso.org/govcourt.4.2.1.html

*Louisiana*
Louisiana Supreme Court          www.lasc.org

*Maine*
Maine State Bar Association          www.mainebar.org/

Judicial Branch          www.courts.state.me.us/

*Maryland*
Maryland State Bar Association          www.msba.org

Court System          www.courts.state.md.us/

*Michigan*
Michigan State Bar Association          www.michbar.org/

Institute of Continuing
Legal Education          www.umich.edu/~icle/

Washtenaw County Trial Court          www.co.washtenaw.mi.us/depts/courts/index.htm

(*This is an excellent site describing the various court functions, Friend of the Court, court schedules, backgrounds of the judges, and an opinion bank of their past opinions, as well as a look at how every court Web site should be designed.*)

*Minnesota*
Minnesota State Court System          www.courts.state.mn.us

*Mississippi*
Mississippi State Bar Association          www.msbar.org/

Supreme Court          www.mslawyer.com/mssc

*Missouri*
Missouri State Bar Association          www.mobar.org/

Supreme Court of Missouri
Home Page          www.osca.state.mo.us

*Montana*
Montana Supreme
Court Options          161.7.121.6/OPININS
>HTM[sic]

*Nebraska*
Nebraska State Bar Association          www.nol.org/legal/nsba/

*New Hampshire*
New Hampshire State          www.nh.com/legal/nhbar/
Bar Association

Judicial Branch of New Hampshire          www.state.nh.us/courts/
State Government          home.htm

*New Jersey*
New Jersey State          www.njsba.com/
Bar Association

Rutgers Law School-Camden,          www-camlaw.rutgers.
Opinions of New Jersey Courts          edu/cgi-bin/decisions/
          search.pl

*New Mexico*
Second Judicial District Court          www.cabq.gov/cjnet/ds2alb/
of New Mexico

*New York*
New York State Bar Association          www.nysba.org/

New York State Court          204.97.2.107/ucscoa.html
of Appeals

*North Carolina*
North Carolina State          www.barlinc.org/
Bar Association

The Judicial Branch in          www.aoc.state.nc.us/www/
North Carolina—Official          courts/index.html
Home Page

*North Dakota*
The North Dakota Supreme          sc3.court.state.nd.us/
Court Home Page

*Ohio*
Ohio Government Judicial Page          winslo.ohio.gov/stgvjud.html

*Oklahoma*
Oklahoma Public Legal          www.onenet.net/okgov/
Research System

*Oregon*
Oregon Law and Resources

www.willamette.edu/law/
longlib/truman/oregon.htm

*Pennsylvania*
Pennsylvania Bar Association

www.pa-bar.org/www.legalcom.

Pennsylvania Courts on the
Web compiled by Legal
Communications

com/courts.htm

*Rhode Island*
Rhode Island State
Bar Association

www.ribar.com/

Rhode Island Court Resources

www.ribar.com/Courts/
courts.html

*South Carolina*
Opinions of the Supreme
Court of South Carolina

www.law.sc.edu/opinions/
options.htm

*South Dakota*
South Dakota State
Bar Association

www.sdbar.org/

South Dakota Supreme
Court Opinions

www.sdbar.org/opinions/
index.htm

*Tennessee*
Tennessee State Bar Association

www.tba.org/

Supreme Court Opinions
and Rules (WordPerfect for
Windows format)

www.tc.state.tn.us/opinions/
tsc/opsttsc.htm

*Utah*
Utah State Bar Association

www.utahbar.org/

Utah State Court System
Home Page

courtlink.utcourts.gov/

*Vermont*
Vermont Bar Association

www.vtbar.org/

Vermont Judiciary Home Page

www.state.vt.us/courts

*Virginia*
Virginia State Bar Association          www.vsb.org/

Opinions of the Supreme                 www.vacle.org/opinions/
Court of Virginia                       caselist.htm

*Washington*
Washington State Bar Association        www.wsba.org/

Supreme Court Opinions                  www.cdlaw.com/cases.htm

*West Virginia*
West Virginia State                     www.wvba.org/
Bar Association

Supreme Court of Appeals                www.state.wv.us/wvsca

*Wisconsin*
Wisconsin State Bar                      www.wisbar.org/home.htm
Association (WISBAR)

Wisconsin Legal Information             www.wisbar.org/lr-menu.htm
(from WISBAR)

*Wyoming*
Supreme Court Opinions                  courts.state.wy.us/OPINION
                                        >HTM


*Federal/National Sites*
Federal Office of Child                 www.acf.dhhs.gov/programs/
Support Enforcement                     cse/index.html

# RESOURCE GROUPS

There are literally thousands of resource groups around the country. Some are chapters of national groups and others are strictly local. You can usually get referrals to groups in your area by looking under "Counseling Services" in the yellow pages or by contacting your local community services agency or church. If you have Internet access, many services are available online by state. Otherwise, you can try contacting one of the resources I have listed below and ask to be referred to an appropriate group or organization in your area. Always ask about fees charged, if any, and be careful to read any agreement that you sign.

## Financial Resources

ASI Credit Reports and Information
Tel. (800) 864-7729
This company offers a copy of your (or your spouse's) credit report for $24.95. Find out the real condition of your credit.

Debt Counselors of America
Tel. (800) 680-3328
Web site *www.DCA.org*
A national company that can help you get your finances in order for a fee. Sometimes a good alternative to bankruptcy, but be sure you understand the fees you will be charged.

National Foundation for Consumer Credit
8611 Second Avenue, Suite 100
Silver Spring, MD 20910
Tel. (800) 388-2227

National Resource Network
3631 Fairmont
Dallas, TX 75219
Tel. (214) 528-9080

Pension Appraisers, Inc.
P.O. Box 4396
Allentown, PA 18105
Tel. (800) 447-0084

Pension Rights Center
918 16th Street NW, Suite 704
Washington, D.C. 20006
Tel. (202) 296-3776
    It is always a good idea to know the value of your pension and the
conditions and terms attached to it.

## Psychological and Support Groups

American Association for Marriage and Family Therapy
1100 17th Street NW, Tenth Floor
Washington, D.C. 20036
Tel. (800) 374-2638

American Self-Help Clearing House
St. Clare-Riverside Medical Center
Denville, NJ 07834
Tel. (201) 625-7101

Divorce Anonymous
2600 Colorado Avenue, Suite 270
Santa Monica, CA 90404
Tel. (310) 998-6538

Divorce Support
5020 West School Street
Chicago, IL 60641
Tel. (312) 286-4541

International Association for Marriage and Family Counselors
c/o American Counseling Association
5999 Stevenson Avenue
Alexandria, VA 22302
Tel. (800) 545-AACD

Joint Custody Association
10606 Wilkins Avenue
Los Angeles, CA 90024
Tel. (310) 475-5352

North American Conference of Separated and Divorced Catholics
80 Saint Mary's Drive
Cranston, RI 02920
Tel. (401) 943-7903

Older Women's League
666 11th Street, Suite 700
Washington, D.C. 20001
Tel. (202) 783-6686

## Fathers' Groups

American Coalition for Fathers and Children (ACFC)
2000 Pennsylvania Avenue NW, Suite 148
Washington, D.C. 20006
Web site *www.scfc.org*
    The ACFC has links on its Web page to other fathers rights groups
and maintains an active lobbying arm.

Dads Against Discrimination
320 SW Stark, #516
Portland, OR 97204
1-503-222-1111

Father's Rights and Equality Exchange
701 Welch Road #323
Palo Alto, CA 94304

National Congress for Fathers and Children
P.O. Box 171675
Kansas City, KS 66117-1675
Tel. (800) 733-3237
    This fee-based membership organization seems to be associated
with Fathers for Equal Rights.

National Fatherhood Initiative
600 Eden Road, Building E
Lancaster, PA 17601
Tel. (800) 790-3237

Parents Without Partners
8807 Colesville Road
Silver Spring, MD 20910
Tel. (800) 637-7974

## Women's Groups

Committee for Mother and Child Rights
210 Old Orchard Drive
Clear Brook, VA 22624-1647
Tel. (540) 722-3652

Mothers Without Custody
P.O. Box 27418
Houston, TX 77227
Tel. (713) 840-1622

National Center of Women and Family Law
275 Seventh Avenue, Suite 1206
New York, NY 10001
Tel. (212) 741-9480

National Organization of Single Mothers
P.O. Box 68
Midland, NC 28107-0068
Tel. (704) 888-5437

National Organization for Women
1000 16th Street NW, Suite 700
Washington, D.C. 20036
Tel. (202) 331-0066
Web site *www.now.org*

National Women's Law Center
11 Dupont Circle NW, Suite 800
Washington, D.C. 20036
Tel. (202) 588-5180

Parents Without Partners
8807 Colesville Road
Silver Spring, MD 20910
Tel. (800) 637-7974

Women's Law Project
125 South 9th Street, Suite 401
Philadelphia, PA 19107
Tel. (215) 928-9801

Women's Legal Defense Fund
1825 Connecticut Avenue NW, Suite 710
Washington, D.C. 20001
Tel. (202) 986-2600

## Child Custody, Child Support, Missing Children

Association for Children for Enforcement of Support
2260 Upton Avenue
Toledo, OH 43606

Children's Rights Council
220 I Street NE, Suite 200
Washington, D.C. 20002
Tel. (202) 547-6227

Federal Office of Child Enforcement
370 L'Enfant Promenade SW
Washington, D.C. 20447
Web site www.acf.dhhs.gov/programs/cse/

Find the Children
11811 West Olympic Boulevard
Los Angeles, CA 90064
Tel. (310) 477-6721

Mothers Without Custody
P.O. Box 27418
Houston, TX 77227
Tel. (713) 840-1622

National Association of Child Advocates
1522 K Street NW, Suite 600
Washington, D.C. 20005
Tel. (202) 289-0777

National Association of Counsel for Children
1205 Oneida Street
Denver, CO 80220
Tel. (303) 322-2260
    Includes attorney referrals in your area.

National Center for Missing or Exploited Children
2101 Wilson Boulevard, Suite 550
Arlington, VA 22201
Tel. (800) 826-7653

Organization for Enforcement of Child Support
1712 Deer Park Road
Finksburg, MD 21048
Tel. (410) 876-1826

## Domestic Violence Resources

AMEND (Abusive Men Exploring New Directions)
777 Grant Street, Suite 60
Denver, CO 80203

CALM (Child Abuse Listening and Mediation)
P.O. Box 90754
Santa Barbara, CA 93190
Tel. (805) 965-2376

Child Welfare League of America
440 1st Street NW, Suite 310
Washington, D.C. 20001
Tel. (202) 638-2952

Pennsylvania Coalition Against Domestic Violence
Tel. (800) 537-2238
    Not just for Pennsylvania, this is a national resource.

Additionally, you can call your local prosecutor or state's attorney office. There are safe houses available in many areas
without cost. The women's rights groups will also be of great
assistance.

# THE UNIFORM INTERSTATE FAMILY SUPPORT ACT (UIFSA)

**P**rior to the enactment of UIFSA, all states had adopted either the Uniform Reciprocal Enforcement of Support Act (URESA) or the Revised Uniform Reciprocal Enforcement of Support Act (RURESA). The purpose of these acts was to make the collection of child support easier between states when the payer was residing in a different state than the one where the court had ordered the support. Theoretically, the acts were supposed to make collection easier and cheaper since a person entitled to support did not have to travel to the other state and hire a private attorney to file suit against the payer.

In reality, the URESA acts were largely ineffective. Their primary fault was in the ability of the other state to legally modify the support order entered by the original state. This created two court systems assuming jurisdiction over the same matter, which created much conflict. In one case I handled, the original court cancelled the support obligation altogether since my client had assumed custody, but it took over a year to get the foreign state to recognize the cancellation of support and stop collecting the payments from my client.

In response to the problems of URESA, the federal government introduced UIFSA. This model statute has now been adopted by the majority of states (primarily because of the financial incentives the government attached to its adoption). Under UIFSA there is only one court that can modify the original order. The reciprocal state is in merely a collection role, with the means of collection and enforcing the order greatly simplified. For instance, under UIFSA the originating state can send an income withholding order directly to the employer of the payer in the foreign state and the employer is bound to follow it. It is still possible to transfer jurisdiction to another state, but only if the parties both agree or if neither of them live in the original state.

The following is a copy of the uniform statute as adopted by the state of Wyoming:

## Uniform Interstate Family Support Act (UIFSA)

### 20-4-139. Short title.
This act may be cited as the "Uniform Interstate Family Support Act."

### 20-4-140. Definitions.
(a) As used in this act:

(i)    "Child" means an individual, whether over or under the age of majority, who is or is alleged to be owed a duty of support by the individual's parent who is or is alleged to be the beneficiary of a support order directed to the parent;

(ii)    "Child support order" means a support order for a child, including a child who has attained the age of majority under the law of the issuing state;

(iii)    "Duty of support" means an obligation imposed or imposable by law to provide support for a child, spouse or former spouse, including an unsatisfied obligation to provide support;

(iv)    "Home state" means the state in which a child lived with a parent or a person acting as a parent for at least six (6) consecutive months immediately preceding the time of filing of a petition or comparable pleading for support and, if a child less than six (6) months old, the state in which the child lived from birth with any of them. A period of temporary absence of any of them is counted as part of the six (6) month or other period;

(v)    "Income" includes earnings or other periodic entitlements to money from any source and any other property subject to withholding for support under the law of this state;

(vi)    "Income withholding order" means an order or other legal process directed to an obligor's employer or other payor, as defined by the Income Withholding Act, W. S. 20-6-201 through 20-6-222, to withhold support from the income of the obligor;

(vii)    "Initiating state" means a state from which a proceeding is filed for forwarding to a responding state under the Uniform Interstate Family Support Act or a law or procedure substantially similar to this act, the

Uniform Reciprocal Enforcement of Support Act, or the Revised Uniform Reciprocal Enforcement of Support Act;

(viii) "Initiating tribunal" means the authorized tribunal in an initiating state;

(ix) "Issuing state" means the state in which a tribunal issues a support order or renders a judgment determining parentage;

(x) "Issuing tribunal" means the tribunal that issues a support order or renders a judgment determining parentage;

(xi) "Obligee" means:

(A) An individual to whom a duty of support is or is alleged to be owed or in whose favor a support order has been issued or a judgment determining parentage has been rendered;

(B) A state or political subdivision to which the rights under a duty of support or support order have been assigned or which has independent claims based on financial assistance provided to an individual obligee; or

(C) An individual seeking a judgment determining parentage of the individual's child.

(xii) "Obligor" means an individual, or the estate of a decedent:

(A) Who owes or is alleged to owe a duty of support;

(B) Who is alleged but has not been adjudicated to be a parent of a child; or

(C) Who is liable under a support order.

(xiii) "Register" means to record or file a support order or judgment determining parentage in the appropriate location for the recording or filing of foreign judgments generally or foreign support orders specifically;

(xiv) "Registering tribunal" means a tribunal in which a support order is registered;

(xv) "Responding state" means a state in which a proceeding is filed or to which a proceeding is forwarded for filing from an initiating state under the Uniform Interstate Family Support Act or a law or procedure substantially similar to this act, the Uniform Reciprocal Enforcement of Support Act, or the Revised Uniform Reciprocal Enforcement of Support Act;

(xvi) "Responding tribunal" means the authorized tribunal in a responding state;

(xvii) "Spousal support order" means a support order for a spouse or former spouse of the obligor;

(xviii) "State" means a state of the United States, the District of Columbia, the United States Virgin Islands, or any territory or insular possession subject to the jurisdiction of the United States. The term includes:

(A) An Indian tribe; and

(B) A foreign jurisdiction that has enacted a law or established procedures for issuance and enforcement of support orders which are substantially similar to the procedures under this act, the Uniform Reciprocal Enforcement of Support Act, or the Revised Uniform Reciprocal Enforcement of Support Act.

(xix)   "Support enforcement agency" means a public official or agency authorized to seek:
- (A) Enforcement of support orders or laws relating to the duty of support;
- (B) Establishment or modification of child support;
- (C) Determination of parentage; or
- (D) To locate obligors or their assets.

(xx)   "Support order" means a judgment, decree, or order, whether temporary, final, or subject to modification, for the benefit of a child, a spouse, or a former spouse, which provides for monetary support, health care, arrearages or reimbursement, and may include related costs and fees, interest, income withholding, attorney's fees, and other relief;

(xxi)   "Tribunal" means a court, administrative agency or quasi-judicial entity authorized to establish, enforce or modify support orders or to determine parentage. For purposes of establishing, enforcing or modifying support orders or determining parentage in Wyoming, tribunal means only the district court;

(xxii)   "This act" means W. S. 20-4-139 through 20-4-192;

(xxiii)   "IV-D agency" means the department of family services;

(xxiv)   "Law" includes decisional and statutory law and rules and regulations having the force of law.

## 20-4-141. Remedies cumulative.
Remedies provided by the Uniform Interstate Family Support Act are cumulative and do not affect the availability of remedies under other law.

## 20-4-142. Basis for jurisdiction over nonresident.
(a) In a proceeding to establish, enforce, or modify a support order or to determine parentage, a tribunal of this state may exercise personal jurisdiction over a nonresident individual or the individual's guardian or conservator if:

(i)   The individual is personally served with notice within the state;

(ii)   The individual submits to the jurisdiction of this state by consent, by entering a general appearance, or by filing a responsive document having the effect of waiving any contest to personal jurisdiction;

(iii)   The individual resided with the child in this state;

(iv)   The individual resided in this state and provided prenatal expenses or support for the child;

(v)   The child resides in this state as a result of the act or directives of the individual;

(vi)   The individual engaged in sexual intercourse in this state and the child may have been conceived by that act of intercourse;

(vii)   The individual asserted parentage in this state pursuant to W. S. 14-2-101 through 14-2-120;

(viii)   There is any other basis consistent with the constitutions of this state and the United States for the exercise of personal jurisdiction.

**20-4-143. Procedure when exercising jurisdiction over nonresident.**
A tribunal of this state exercising personal jurisdiction over a nonresident under W. S. 20-4-142 may apply to receive evidence from another state under W. S. 20-4-166 and to obtain discovery through a tribunal of another state under W. S. 20-4-168. In all other respects, W. S. 20-4-151 through 20-4-179 do not apply and the tribunal shall apply the procedural and substantive law of this state, including the rules on choice of law other than those established by the Uniform Interstate Family Support Act.

**20-4-144. Initiating and responding tribunal of this state.**
Under the Uniform Interstate Family Support Act, a tribunal of this state may serve as an initiating tribunal to forward proceedings to another state and as a responding tribunal for proceedings initiated in another state.

**20-4-145. Simultaneous proceedings in another state.**
(a) A tribunal of this state may exercise jurisdiction to establish a support order if the petition or comparable pleading is filed after a pleading is filed in another state only if:

    (i)    The petition or comparable pleading in this state is filed before the expiration of the time allowed in the other state for filing a responsive pleading challenging the exercise of jurisdiction by the other state;

    (ii)    The contesting party timely challenges the exercise of jurisdiction in the other state; and

    (iii)    If relevant, this state is the home state of the child.

(b) A tribunal of this state may not exercise jurisdiction to establish a support order if the petition or comparable pleading is filed before a petition or comparable pleading is filed in another state if:

    (i)    The petition or comparable pleading in the other state is filed before the expiration of the time allowed in this state for filing a responsive pleading challenging the exercise of jurisdiction by this state;

    (ii)    The contesting party timely challenges the exercise of jurisdiction in this state;

    (iii)    If relevant, the other state is the home state of the child.

**20-4-146. Continuing exclusive jurisdiction.**
(a) A tribunal of this state issuing a support order consistent with the law of this state has continuing, exclusive jurisdiction over a child support order:

    (i)    As long as this state remains the residence of the obligor, the individual obligee or the child for whose benefit the support order is issued; or

    (ii)    Until all of the parties who are individuals have filed written consents with the tribunal of this state for a tribunal of another state to modify the order and assume continuing, exclusive jurisdiction.

(b) A tribunal of this state issuing a child support order consistent with the law of this state may not exercise its continuing jurisdiction to modify the order if the order has been modified by a tribunal of another state pursuant to a law substantially similar to the Uniform Interstate Family Support Act.

(c) If a child support order of this state is modified by a tribunal of another state pursuant to this act or a law substantially similar to this act, a tribunal of this state loses its continuing, exclusive jurisdiction with regard to prospective enforcement of the order issued in this state, and may only:

    (i)    Enforce the order that was modified as the amounts accruing before the modification;

    (ii)    Enforce nonmodifiable aspects of that order; and

    (iii)    Provide other appropriate relief for violations of that order which occurred before the effective date of the modification.

(d) A tribunal of this state shall recognize the continuing, exclusive jurisdiction of a tribunal of another state which has issued a child support order pursuant to this act or a law substantially similar to this act.

(e) A temporary support order issued ex parte or pending resolution of a jurisdictional conflict does not create continuing, exclusive jurisdiction in the issuing tribunal.

(f) A tribunal of this state issuing a support order consistent with the law of this state has continuing, exclusive jurisdiction over a spousal support order throughout the existence of the support obligation. A tribunal of this state may not modify a spousal support order issued by a tribunal of another state having continuing, exclusive jurisdiction over that order under the law of that state.

**20-4-147. Enforcement and modification of support order by tribunal having continuing jurisdiction.**

(a) A tribunal of this state may serve as an initiating tribunal to request a tribunal of another state to enforce or modify a support order issued in that state.

(b) A tribunal of this state having continuing, exclusive jurisdiction over a support order may act as a responding tribunal to enforce or modify the order. If a party subject to the continuing, exclusive jurisdiction of the tribunal no longer resides in the issuing state, in subsequent proceedings the tribunal may apply to receive evidence from another state under W. S. 20-4-166 and to obtain discovery through a tribunal of another state under W. S. 20-4-168.

(c) A tribunal of this state which lacks continuing, exclusive jurisdiction over a spousal support order may not serve as a responding tribunal to modify a spousal support order of another state.

**20-4-148. Recognition of controlling child support orders.**
(a) If a proceeding is brought under this act and only one (1) tribunal has issued a child support order, the order of that tribunal shall be so recognized.
  (i)    Repealed By Laws 1998, ch. 97, §3.
  (ii)   Repealed By Laws 1998, ch. 97, §3.
  (iii)  Repealed By Laws 1998, ch. 97, §3.
  (iv)   Repealed By Laws 1998, ch. 97, §3.

(b) If a proceeding is brought under this act, and two (2) or more child support orders have been issued by tribunals of this state or another state with regard to the same obligor and child, a tribunal of this state shall apply the following rules in determining which order to recognize for purposes of continuing, exclusive jurisdiction:
  (i)    If only one (1) of the tribunals would have continuing, exclusive jurisdiction under this act, the order of that tribunal controls and shall be so recognized.
  (ii)   If more than one (1) of the tribunals would have continuing, exclusive jurisdiction under this act, an order issued by a tribunal in the current home state of the child controls and shall be so recognized, but if an order has not been issued in the current home state of the child the order most recently issued controls and shall be so recognized.

**20-4-149. Multiple child support orders for two or more obligees.**
In responding to multiple registrations or petitions for enforcement of two (2) or more child support orders in effect at the same time with regard to the same obligor and different individual obligees, at least one (1) of which was issued by a tribunal of another state, a tribunal of this state shall enforce those orders in the same manner as if the multiple orders had been issued by a tribunal of this state.

**20-4-150. Credit for payments.**
Amounts collected and credited for a particular period pursuant to a support order issued by a tribunal of another state shall be credited against the amounts accruing or accrued for the same period under a support order issued by the tribunal of this state.

**20-4-151. Proceedings under the Uniform Interstate Family Support Act.**
(a) Except as otherwise provided in this act, W. S. 20-4-151 through 20-4-169 apply to all proceedings under the Uniform Interstate Family Support Act.

(b) The Uniform Interstate Family Support Act provides for the following proceedings:
  (i)    Establishment of an order for spousal support or child support pursuant to W. S. 20-4-170;

(ii)    Enforcement of a support order and income withholding order of another state without registration pursuant to W. S. 20-4-171, 20-4-172 and 20-4-190 through 20-4-192;

(iii)    Registration of an order for spousal support or child support of another state for enforcement pursuant to W. S. 20-4-173 through 20-4-184, 20-4-193 and 20-4-194;

(iv)    Modification of an order for child support or spousal support issued by a district court of this state pursuant to W. S. 20-4-144 through 20-4-147;

(v)    Registration of an order for child support of another state for modification pursuant to W. S. 20-4-173 through 20-4-184, 20-4-193 and 20-4-194;

(vi)    Determination of parentage pursuant to W. S. 20-4-185; and

(vii)    Assertion of jurisdiction over nonresidents pursuant to W. S. 20-4-142 and 20-4-143.

(c) An individual petitioner or a support enforcement agency may commence a proceeding authorized under the act by filing a petition in an initiating tribunal for forwarding to a responding tribunal or by filing a petition or a comparable pleading directly in a tribunal of another state which has or can obtain personal jurisdiction over the respondent.

**20-4-152. Action by minor parent.**
A minor parent, or a guardian or other legal representative of a minor parent, may maintain a proceeding on behalf of, or for the benefit of, the minor's child.

**20-4-153. Application of law of this state.**
(a) Except as otherwise provided by the Uniform Interstate Family Support Act, a responding tribunal of this state:

(i)    Shall apply the procedural and substantive law, including the rules on choice of law, generally applicable to similar proceedings originating in this state and may exercise all powers and provide all remedies available in those proceedings; and

(ii)    Shall determine the duty of support and the amount payable in accordance with the presumptive child support established under W. S. 20-6-304.

**20-4-154. Duties of initiating tribunal.**
(a) Upon the filing of a petition authorized by the Uniform Interstate Family Support Act, an initiating tribunal of this state shall forward three (3) copies of the petition and its accompanying documents:

(i)    To the responding tribunal or appropriate support enforcement agency in the responding state; or

(ii)    If the identity of the responding tribunal is unknown, to the state information agency of the responding state with a request that they be forwarded to the appropriate tribunal and that receipt be acknowledged.

(b) If a responding state has not enacted this act or a law or procedure substantially similar to this act, a tribunal of this state may issue a certificate or other document and make findings required by the law of the responding state. If the responding state is a foreign jurisdiction, the tribunal may specify the amount of support sought and provide other documents necessary to satisfy the requirements of the responding state.

### 20-4-155. Duties and power of responding tribunal.

(a) When a responding tribunal of this state receives a petition or comparable pleading from initiating tribunal or directly pursuant to W. S. 20-4-151(c), it shall cause the petition or pleading to be filed and notify the petitioner where and when it was filed.

(b) A responding tribunal of this state, to the extent otherwise authorized by law, may do one (1) or more of the following:

    (i)    Issue or enforce a support order, modify a child support order or render a judgment to determine parentage;

    (ii)    Order an obligor to comply with a support order, specifying the amount and manner of compliance;

    (iii)    Medical support, whether in the form of periodic cash payment, stated as a sum certain, or ordering the obligor to provide health insurance coverage for the child under a policy available through the obligor's employment;

    (iv)    Determine the amount of any arrearages, and specify a method of payment;

    (v)    Enforce orders by civil or criminal contempt, or both;

    (vi)    Set aside property for satisfaction of the support order;

    (vii)    Place liens and order execution on the obligor's property;

    (viii)    Order an obligor to keep the tribunal informed of the obligor's current residential address, telephone number, employer, address of employment and telephone number at the place of employment;

    (ix)    Issue a bench warrant for an obligor who has failed after proper notice to appear at a hearing ordered by the tribunal and enter the warrant in any local and state computer system for criminal warrants;

    (x)    Order the obligor to seek appropriate employment by specified methods;

    (xi)    Award reasonable attorney's fees and other fees and court costs;

    (xii)    Repealed By Laws 1998, ch. 97, 3.

    (xiii)    Grant any other available remedy.

(c) A responding tribunal of this state shall include in a support order issued under the Uniform Interstate Family Support Act, or in the documents accompanying the order, the calculations on which the support order is based.

(d) A responding tribunal of this state may not condition the payment of a support order issued under this act upon compliance by a party with provisions for visitation.

(e) If a responding tribunal of this state issues an order under this act, the tribunal shall send a copy of the order to the petitioner and the respondent and to the initiating tribunal, if any.

## 20-4-156. Inappropriate tribunal.

If a petition or comparable pleading is received by an inappropriate tribunal of this state, it shall forward the pleading and accompanying document to an appropriate tribunal in this state or another state and notify the petitioner where and when the pleading was sent.

## 20-4-157. Duties of support enforcement agency.

(a) A support enforcement agency of this state, upon request, shall provide services to a petitioner in a proceeding under this act.

(b) A support enforcement agency that is providing services to the petitioner as appropriate shall:

(i)     Take all steps necessary to enable an appropriate tribunal in this state or another state to obtain jurisdiction over the respondent;

(ii)     Request an appropriate tribunal to set a date, time and place for a hearing;

(iii)     Make a reasonable effort to obtain all relevant information, including information as to income and property of the parties;

(iv)     Within five (5) days, exclusive of Saturdays, Sundays and legal holidays, after receipt of a written notice from an initiating, responding or registering tribunal, send a copy of the notice to the petitioner;

(v)     Within five (5) days, exclusive of Saturdays, Sundays and legal holidays, after receipt of a written communication from the respondent or the respondent's attorney, send a copy of the communication to the petitioner; and

(vi)     Notify the petitioner if jurisdiction over the respondent cannot be obtained.

(c) This act does not create or negate a relationship of attorney and client or other fiduciary relationship between a support enforcement agency or the attorney for the agency and the individual being assisted by the agency.

## 20-4-158. Duty of attorney general.

If the state attorney general determines that the support enforcement agency is neglecting or refusing to provide services to an individual, the attorney general may order the agency to perform its duties under this act or may provide those services directly to the individual.

## 20-4-159. Private counsel.

An individual may employ private counsel to represent the individual in proceedings authorized by this act.

**20-4-160. Duties of state information agency.**
(a) The department of family services child support enforcement section is the state information agency under this act.

(b) The state information agency shall:
 (i) Compile and maintain a current list, including addresses, of the tribunals in this state which have jurisdiction under this act and any support enforcement agencies in this state and transmit a copy to the state information agency of every other state;
 (ii) Maintain a register of tribunals and support enforcement agencies received from other states;
 (iii) Forward to the appropriate tribunal in the place in this state in which the individual obligee or the obligor resides, or in which the obligor's property is believed to be located, all documents concerning a proceeding under this act received from an initiating tribunal or the state information agency of the initiating state; and
 (iv) Obtain information concerning the location of the obligor and the obligor's property within this state not exempt from execution, by such means as postal verification and federal or state locator services, examination of telephone directories, requests for the obligor's address from employer, and examination of governmental records, including, to the extent not prohibited by other law, those relating to real property, vital statistics, law enforcement, taxation, motor vehicles, driver's licenses and social security.

**20-4-161. Pleadings and accompanying documents.**
(a) A petitioner seeking to establish or modify a support order or to determine parentage in a proceeding under this act shall verify the petition. Unless otherwise ordered under W. S. 20-4-162, the petition or accompanying document shall provide, so far as known, the name, residential address and social security numbers of the obligor and the obligee, and the name, sex, residential address, social security number and date of birth of each child for whom support is sought. The petition shall be accompanied by a certified copy of any support order in effect. The petition or accompanying documents may include any other information that may assist in locating or identifying the respondent.

(b) The petition shall specify the relief sought. The petition and accompanying documents shall conform substantially with the requirements imposed by the forms mandated by federal law for use in cases filed by a support enforcement agency.

**20-4-162. Nondisclosure of information in exceptional circumstances.**
Upon a finding, which may be made ex parte, that the health, safety or liberty of a party or child would be unreasonably put at risk by the disclosure of identifying information, or if an existing order so provides, a tribunal

shall order that the address of the child or party or other identifying information not be disclosed in a pleading or other document filed in a proceeding under this act.

## 20-4-163. Costs and fees.

(a) The petitioner may not be required to pay a filing fee or other cost.

(b) If an obligee prevails, a responding tribunal may assess against an obligor filing fees, reasonable attorney's fees, other costs and necessary travel and other reasonable expenses incurred by the obligee and the obligee's witnesses. The tribunal may not assess fees, costs or expenses against the obligee or the support enforcement agency of either the initiating or the responding state, except as provided by other law. Attorney's fees may be taxed as costs, and may be ordered paid directly to the attorney, who may enforce the order in the attorney's own name. Payment of support owed to the obligee has priority over fees, costs and expenses.

(c) The tribunal shall order the payment of costs and reasonable attorney's fees if it determines that a hearing was requested primarily for delay. In a proceeding under W. S. 20-4-173 through 20-4-184, a hearing is presumed to have been requested primarily for delay if a registered support order is confirmed or enforced without change.

## 20-4-164. Limited immunity of petitioner.

(a) Participation by a petitioner in a proceeding before a responding tribunal, whether in person, by private attorney, or through services provided by the support enforcement agency, does not confer personal jurisdiction over the petitioner in another proceeding.

(b) A petitioner is not amenable to service of civil process while physically present in this state to participate in a proceeding under this act.

(c) The immunity granted by this section does not extend to civil litigation based on acts unrelated to a proceeding under this act committed by a party while present in this state to participate in the proceeding.

## 20-4-165. Nonparentage as defense.

A party whose parentage of a child has been previously determined by or pursuant to law may not plead nonparentage as a defense to a proceeding under this act.

## 20-4-166. Special rules of evidence and procedure.

(a) The physical presence of the petitioner in a responding tribunal of this state is not required for the establishment, enforcement or modification of a support order or the rendition of a judgment determining parentage.

(b) A verified petition, affidavit, document substantially complying with federally mandated forms and a document incorporated by reference in any of them, not excluded under the hearsay rule if given in person, is admissible in evidence if given under oath by a party or witness residing in another state.

(c) A copy of the record of child support payments certified as a true copy of the original by the custodian of the record may be forwarded to a responding tribunal. The copy is evidence of facts asserted in it, and is admissible to show whether payments were made.

(d) Copies of bills for testing for parentage, and for prenatal and postnatal health care of the mother and child, furnished to the adverse party at least ten (10) days before trial, are admissible in evidence to prove the amount of the charges billed and that the charges were reasonable, necessary and customary.

(e) Documentary evidence transmitted from another state to a tribunal of this state by telephone, telecopier, or other means that do not provide an original writing may not be excluded from evidence on an objection based on the means of transmission.

(f) In a proceeding under this act, a tribunal of this state may permit a party or witness residing in another state to be deposed or to testify by telephone, audiovisual means or other electronic means at a designated tribunal or other location in that state. A tribunal of this state shall cooperate with tribunals of other states in designating an appropriate location for the deposition or testimony.

(g) If a party called to testify at a civil hearing refuses to answer on the ground that the testimony may be self-incriminating, the trier of fact may draw an adverse inference from the refusal.

(h) A privilege against disclosure of communications between spouses does not apply in a proceeding under the act.

### 20-4-167. Communications between tribunals.
A tribunal of this state may communicate with a tribunal of another state in writing, or by telephone or other means, to obtain information concerning the laws of that state, the legal affect of a judgment, decree or order of that tribunal, and the status of a proceeding in the other state. A tribunal of this state may furnish similar information by similar means to a tribunal of another state.

### 20-4-168. Assistance with discovery.
(a) A tribunal of this state may:

    (i)    Request a tribunal of another state to assist in obtaining discovery; and

(ii)    Upon request, compel a person over whom it has jurisdiction to respond to a discovery order issued by a tribunal of another state.

### 20-4-169. Receipt and disbursement of payments.
A support enforcement agency or tribunal of this state shall disburse promptly any amounts received pursuant to a support order, as directed by the order. The agency or tribunal shall furnish to a requesting party or tribunal of another state a certified statement by the custodian of the record of the amounts and dates of all payments received.

### 20-4-170. Petition to establish support order.
(a) If a support order entitled to recognition under this act has not been issued, a responding tribunal of this state may issue a support order if:
(i)    The individual seeking the order resides in another state; or
(ii)    The support enforcement agency seeking the order is located in another state.

(b) The tribunal may issue a temporary child support order if:
(i)    The respondent has signed a verified statement acknowledging parentage;
(ii)    The respondent has been determined by or pursuant to law to be the parent; or
(iii)    There is other clear and convincing evidence that the respondent is the child's parent.

(c) Upon finding, after notice and opportunity to be heard, that an obligor owes a duty of support, the tribunal shall issue a support order directed to the obligor and may issue other orders pursuant to W. S. 20-4-155.

### 20-4-171. Employer's receipt of income withholding order of another state; employer's compliance with income withholding order of another state; compliance with multiple income withholding orders.
(a) An income withholding order issued in another state may be sent to the person or entity defined as the obligor's employer under W. S. 20-6-201 through 20-6-222 without first filing a petition or comparable pleading or registering the order with a tribunal of this state.
(i)    Repealed By Laws 1998, ch. 97, 3.
(ii)    Repealed By Laws 1998, ch. 97, 3.
(iii)    Repealed By Laws 1998, ch. 97, 3.

(b) Repealed By Laws 1998, ch. 97, 3.

(c) Upon receipt of an income withholding order, the obligor's employer shall immediately provide a copy of the order to the obligor.

(d) The employer shall treat an income withholding order issued in another state which appears regular on its face as if it had been issued by a tribunal of this state.

(e) Except as otherwise provided in subsections (f) and (g), the employer shall withhold and distribute the funds as directed in the withholding order by complying with terms of the order which specify:

(i)     The duration and amount of periodic payments of current child support, stated as a sum certain;

(ii)     The person or agency designated to receive payments and the address to which the payments are to be forwarded;

(iii)     Medical support, whether in the form of periodic cash payment, stated as a sum certain, or ordering the obligor to provide health insurance coverage for the child under a policy available through the obligor's employment;

(iv)     The amount of periodic payments of fees and costs for a support enforcement agency, the issuing tribunal, and the obligee's attorney, stated as sums certain; and

(v)     The amount of periodic payments of arrearages and interest on arrearages, stated as sums certain.

(f) An employer shall comply with the law of the state of the obligor's principal place of employment for withholding from income with respect to:

(i)     The employer's fee for processing an income withholding order;

(ii)     The maximum amount permitted to be withheld from the obligor's income; and

(iii)     The times within which the employer shall implement the withholding order and forward the child support payment.

(g) If an obligor's employer receives multiple income withholding orders with respect to the earnings of the same obligor, the employer satisfies the terms of the multiple orders if the employer complies with the law of the state of the obligor's principal place of employment to establish the priorities for withholding and allocating income withheld for multiple child support obligees.

**20-4-172. Administrative enforcement of orders.**

(a) A party seeking to enforce a support order or an income withholding order, or both, issued by a tribunal of another state may send the documents required for registering the order to a support enforcement agency of this state.

(b) Upon receipt of the documents, the support enforcement agency, without initially seeking to register the order, shall consider and, if appropriate, use any administrative procedure authorized by the law of this state to enforce a support order or an income withholding order, or both. If the obligor does not contest administrative enforcement, the order need not be registered. If the obligor contests the validity or administrative enforcement of the order, the support enforcement agency shall register the order pursuant to the Uniform Interstate Family Support Act.

(c) The department of family services shall adopt rules and regulations consistent with federal requirements to implement this section.

### 20-4-173. Registration of order for enforcement.
A support order or an income withholding order issued by a tribunal of another state may be registered in this state for enforcement.

### 20-4-174. Procedure to register order for enforcement.
(a) A support order or an income withholding order of another state may be registered in this state by sending the following documents and information to the appropriate tribunal in this state:

    (i)    A letter of transmittal to the tribunal requesting registration and enforcement;

    (ii)    Two (2) copies, including one (1) certified copy, of all orders to be registered, including any modification of an order;

    (iii)    A sworn statement by the party seeking registration or a certified statement by the custodian of the records showing the amount of any arrearage;

    (iv)    The name of the obligor and, if known:

        (A) The obligor's address and social security number;

        (B) The name and address of the obligor's employer or other payor and any other source of income of the obligor; and

        (C) A description and the location of property of the obligor in this state not exempt from execution; and

        (D) Repealed By Laws 1998, ch. 97, §3.

    (v)    The name and address of the obligee and, if applicable, the agency or person to whom support payments are to be remitted.

(b) On receipt of a request for registration, the registering tribunal shall cause the order to be filed as a foreign judgment, together with one (1) copy of the documents and information, regardless of their form.

(c) A petition or comparable pleading seeking a remedy that shall be affirmatively sought under other law of this state may be filed at the same time as the request for registration, or later. The pleading shall specify the grounds for the remedy sought.

### 20-4-175. Effect of registration for enforcement.
(a) A support order or income withholding order issued in another state is registered when the order is filed in the registering tribunal of this state.

(b) A registered order issued in another state is enforceable in the same manner and is subject to the same procedures as an order issued by a tribunal of this state.

(c) Except as otherwise provided in W. S. 20-4-173 through 20-4-184, a tribunal of this state shall recognize and enforce, but shall not modify, a registered order if the issuing tribunal had jurisdiction.

**20-4-176. Choice of law.**
(a) The law of the issuing state governs the nature, extent, amount and duration of current payments and other obligations of support and the payment of arrearages under the order.

(b) In a proceeding for arrearages, the statute of limitation under the laws of this state or of the issuing state, whichever is longer, applies.

**20-4-177. Notice of registration of order.**
(a) When a support order or income withholding order issued in another state is registered, the registering tribunal shall notify the nonregistering party. The notice shall be accompanied by a copy of the registered order and the documents and relevant information accompanying the order.

(b) The notice shall inform the nonregistering party:
    (i)    That a registered order is enforceable as of the date of registration in the same manner as an order issued by a tribunal of this state;
    (ii)    That a hearing to contest the validity or enforcement of the registered order shall be requested within twenty (20) days after the date of mailing or personal service of the notice;
    (iii)    That failure to contest the validity or enforcement of the registered order in a timely manner will result in confirmation of the order and enforcement of the order and the alleged arrearages and precludes further contest of that order with respect to any matter that could have been asserted; and (iv) Of the amount of any alleged arrearages.

(c) Upon registration of an income withholding order for enforcement, the registering tribunal shall notify the obligor's employer pursuant to W. S. 20-6-201 through 20-6-222.

**20-4-178. Procedure to contest validity or enforcement of registered order.**
(a) A nonregistering party seeking to contest the validity or enforcement of a registered order in this state shall request a hearing within twenty (20) days after the date of mailing or personal service of notice of the registration. The nonregistering party may seek to vacate the registration, to assert any defense to an allegation of noncompliance with the registered order, or to contest the remedies being sought or the amount of any alleged arrearages pursuant to W. S. 20-4-179.

(b) If the nonregistering party fails to contest the validity or enforcement of the registered order, the registering tribunal shall schedule the matter for hearing and give notice to the parties of the date, time and place of the hearing.

**20-4-179. Contest of registration or enforcement.**
(a) A party contesting the validity or enforcement of a registered order or seeking to vacate the registration has the burden of proving one (1) or more of the following defenses:

(i)    The issuing tribunal lacked personal jurisdiction over the contesting party;

(ii)    The order was obtained by fraud;

(iii)    The order has been vacated, suspended or modified by a later order;

(iv)    The issuing tribunal has stayed the order pending appeal;

(v)    There is a defense under the law of this state to the remedy sought;

(vi)    Full or partial payment has been made; or

(vii)    The statute of limitations under W. S. 20-4-176 precludes enforcement of some or all of the arrearages.

(b) If a party presents evidence establishing a full or partial defense under subsection (a) of this section, a tribunal may stay enforcement of the registered order, continue the proceeding to permit production of additional relevant evidence and issue other appropriate orders. An uncontested portion of the registered order may be enforced by all remedies available under the laws of this state.

(c) If the contesting party does not establish a defense under subsection (a) of this section, the registering tribunal shall issue an order confirming the order.

**20-4-180. Confirmed order.**
Confirmation of a registered order, whether by operation of law or after notice and hearing, precludes further contest of the order with respect to any matter that could have been asserted at the time of registration.

**20-4-181. Procedure to register child support order of another state for modification.**
A party or support enforcement agency seeking to modify, or to modify and enforce, a child support order issued in another state shall register that order in this state in the same manner provided in W. S. 20-4-173 through 20-4-176 if the order has not been registered. A petition for modification may be filed at the same time as a request for registration, or later. The pleading shall specify the grounds for modification.

**20-4-182. Effect of registration for modification.**

A tribunal of this state may enforce a child support order of another state registered for purposes of modification, in the same manner as if the order had been issued by a tribunal of this state, but the registered order may be modified only if the requirements of W. S. 20-4-183 have been met.

**20-4-183. Modification of child support order of another state.**

(a) After a child support order issued in another state has been registered in this state, the responding tribunal of this state may modify that order only if W. S. 20-4-193 does not apply and after notice and hearing it finds that:

(i)     The child, or a party who is an individual, is subject to the personal jurisdiction of the tribunal and all of the parties who are individuals have filed written consents in the issuing tribunal for a tribunal of this state to modify the support order and assume continuing, exclusive jurisdiction over the order. However, if the issuing state is a foreign jurisdiction that has not enacted a law or established procedures substantially similar to the procedures under this act, the consent otherwise required of an individual residing in this state is not required for the tribunal to assume jurisdiction to modify the child support order; or

(ii)    The following requirements are met:

(A) The child, the individual obligee and the obligor do not reside in the issuing state;

(B) A petitioner who is a nonresident of this state seeks modification; and

(C) The respondent is subject to the personal jurisdiction of the tribunal of this state.

(b) Modification of a registered child support order is subject to the same requirements, procedures and defenses that apply to the modification of an order issued by a tribunal of this state and the order may be enforced and satisfied in the same manner.

(c) A tribunal of this state may not modify any aspect of a child support order that may not be modified under the law of the issuing state. If two (2) or more tribunals have issued child support orders for the same obligor and child, the order that controls and shall be so recognized under W. S. 20-4-148 establishes the aspects of the support order which are nonmodifiable.

(d) On issuance of an order modifying a child support order issued in another state, a tribunal of this state becomes the tribunal having continuing, exclusive jurisdiction.

**20-4-184. Recognition of order modified in another state.**

(a) A tribunal of this state shall recognize a modification of its earlier child support order by a tribunal of another state which assumed jurisdiction pursuant to this act or a law substantially similar to the Uniform Interstate Family Support Act and, upon request, except as otherwise provided in this act, shall:

(i)    Enforce the order that was modified only as to amounts accruing before the modification;

(ii)    Enforce only nonmodifiable aspects of that order;

(iii)    Provide other appropriate relief only for violations of that order which occurred before the effective date of the modification; and

(iv)    Recognize the modifying order of the other state, upon registration, for the purpose of enforcement.

## 20-4-185. Proceeding to determine parentage.

(a) A tribunal of this state may serve as an initiating or responding tribunal in a proceeding brought under the Uniform Interstate Family Support Act or a law or procedure substantially similar to this act, the Uniform Reciprocal Enforcement of Support Act or the Revised Uniform Reciprocal Enforcement of Support Act to determine that the petitioner is a parent of a particular child or to determine that a respondent is a parent of that child.

(b) In a proceeding to determine parentage, a responding tribunal of this state shall apply the provisions of W. S. 14-2-101 through 14-2-120 and the rules of this state on choice of law.

## 20-4-186. Grounds for rendition.

(a) For purposes of W. S. 20-4-186 and 20-4-187, "governor" includes an individual performing the functions of the governor or the executive authority of a state covered by the Uniform Interstate Family Support Act.

(b) The governor of this state may:

(i)    Demand that the governor of another state surrender an individual found in the other state who is charged criminally in this state with having failed to provide for the support of an obligee; or

(ii)    On the demand by the governor of another state surrender an individual found in this state who is charged criminally in the other state with having failed to provide for the support of an obligee.

(c) A provision for extradition of individuals not inconsistent with this act applies to the demand even if the individual whose surrender is demanded was not in the demanding state when the crime was allegedly committed and has not fled therefrom.

## 20-4-187. Conditions of rendition.

(a) Before making demand that the governor of another state surrender an individual charged criminally in this state with having failed to provide for the support of an obligee, the governor of this state may require a prosecutor of this state to demonstrate that at least sixty (60) days previously the obligee had initiated proceedings for support pursuant to the Interstate Family Support Act or that the proceeding would be of no avail.

(b) If, under the Uniform Interstate Family Support Act or a law substantially similar to this act, the Uniform Reciprocal Enforcement of Support Act or the Revised Uniform Reciprocal Enforcement of Support Act, the governor of another state makes a demand that the governor of this state surrender an individual charged criminally in that state with having failed to provide for the support of a child or other individual to whom a duty of support is owed, the governor may require a prosecutor to investigate the demand and report whether a proceeding for support has been initiated or would be effective. If it appears that a proceeding would be effective but has not been initiated, the governor may delay honoring the demand for a reasonable time to permit the initiation of a proceeding.

(c) If a proceeding for support has been initiated and the individual whose rendition is demanded prevails, the governor may decline to honor the demand. If the petitioner prevails and the individual whose rendition is demanded is subject to a support order, the governor may decline to honor the demand if the individual is complying with the support order.

**20-4-188. Uniformity of application and construction.**
The Uniform Interstate Family Support Act shall be applied and construed to effectuate its general purpose to make uniform the law with respect to the subject of this act among states enacting it.

**20-4-189. Pending action or proceeding under Revised Uniform Reciprocal Enforcement of Support Act; law applicable.**
Any action or proceeding under the Uniform Reciprocal Enforcement of Support Act pending on July 1, 1995, shall continue under the provisions of such act until the court rules on any pending action or proceeding.

**20-4-190. Immunity from civil liability.**
An employer who complies with an income withholding order issued in another state in accordance with this article is not subject to civil liability to an individual or agency with regard to the employer's withholding of child support from the obligor's income.

**20-4-191. Penalties for noncompliance.**
An employer who willfully fails to comply with an income withholding order issued by another state and received for enforcement is subject to the same penalties that may be imposed for noncompliance with an order issued by a tribunal of this state.

**20-4-192. Contest by obligor.**
(a) An obligor may contest the validity or enforcement of an income with-holding order issued in another state and received directly by an employer in this state in the same manner as if the order had been issued by a tribunal of this state. W. S. 20-4-176 applies to the contest.

(b) The obligor shall give notice of the contest to:
    (i)    A support enforcement agency providing services to the obligee;
    (ii)    Each employer that has directly received an income withholding order; and
    (iii)    The person or agency designated to receive payments in the income withholding order or if no person or agency is designated, to the obligee.

**20-4-193. Jurisdiction to modify child support order of another state when individual parties reside in this state.**
(a) If all of the parties who are individuals reside in this state and the child does not reside in the issuing state, a tribunal of this state has jurisdiction to enforce and to modify the issuing state's child support order in a proceeding to register that order.

(b) A tribunal of this state exercising jurisdiction under this section shall apply the provisions of W. S. 20-4-139 through 20-4-143, 20-4-173 through 20-4-184, 20-4-193, 20-4-194, and the procedural and substantive law of this state to the proceeding for enforcement or modification. W. S. 20-4-151 through 20-4-172, 20-4-185 through 20-4-187 and 20-4-190 through 20-4-192 do not apply.

**20-4-194. Notice to issuing tribunal of modification.**
Within thirty (30) days after issuance of a modified child support order, the party obtaining the modification shall file a certified copy of the order with the issuing tribunal that had continuing, exclusive jurisdiction over the earlier order, and in each tribunal in which the party knows the earlier order has been registered. A party who obtains the order and fails to file a certified copy is subject to appropriate sanctions by a tribunal in which the issue of failure to file arises. The failure to file does not affect the validity or enforceability of the modified order of the new tribunal having continuing, exclusive jurisdiction.

# SAMPLE DIVORCE
# FEE AGREEMENT

THE UNDERSIGNED, _____,
referred to herein as "attorney" and,
_____ referred to herein as "client,"
agree as follows:

1. Attorney agrees to represent client in the following legal matter:

Divorce proceedings in _____
[county, state]

2. In consideration of the legal services to be performed, client has paid a retainer to attorney of $_____. Attorney will provide client with an itemized billing from time to time, charging for legal services, including telephone calls, at the rate of $_____ per hour, to be charged against retainer. Additional amounts billed over the retainer will be immediately paid by client. Attorney will provide to client on a monthly basis or more often an itemized listing of time spent on the client's behalf including the date of the service, a description of what was done, and the amount of time billed for that service.

3. Either party may terminate the attorney-client relationship at any time upon notice to the other party.

4. Attorney has made no promises or guarantees other than those contained in writing signed by him as to the outcome of client's case.

5. Client will be responsible for any court costs, deposition fees, expert witness fees, deposition and transcript costs, investigation costs, or other necessary costs expended by attorney of behalf of client's case which amount will be added to client's billing after first being deducted from any retainer for costs.

6. Client understands that billings are due when received.

7. Attorney will keep client regularly informed as to the progress of the case and provide client with copies of all documents and correspondence.

Dated: _____

_____          _____
            Attorney                                    Client

# THE UNIFORM CHILD CUSTODY JURISDICTION ACT (UCCJA)

As Adopted by the State of California

3400. This part may be cited as the Uniform Child Custody Jurisdiction Act.

3401. (a) The general purposes of this part are to:

(1) Avoid jurisdiction competition and conflict with courts of other states in matters of child custody which have in the past resulted in the shifting of children from state to state with harmful effects on their well-being.

(2) Promote cooperation with the courts of other states to the end that a custody decree is rendered in that state which can best decide the case in the interest of the child.

(3) Assure that litigation concerning the custody of a child take place ordinarily in the state with which the child and the child's family have the closest connection and where significant evidence concerning the child's care, protection, training, and personal relationships is most readily available, and that courts of this state decline the exercise of jurisdiction when the child and the child's family have a closer connection with another state.

(4) Discourage continuing controversies over child custody in the interest of greater stability of home environment and of secure family relationships for the child.

(5) Deter abductions and other unilateral removals of children undertaken to obtain custody awards.

(6) Avoid relitigation of custody decisions of other states in this state insofar as feasible.

(7) Facilitate the enforcement of custody decrees of other states.

(8) Promote and expand the exchange of information and other forms of mutual assistance between the courts of this state and those of other states concerned with the same child.

(b) This part shall be construed to promote the general purposes stated in this section.

3402. As used in this part:

(a) "Contestant" means a person, including a parent, who claims a right to custody or visitation rights with respect to a child.

(b) "Custody determination" means a court decision and court orders and instructions providing for the custody of a child, including visitation rights; it does not include a decision relating to child support or any other monetary obligation of any person.

(c) "Custody proceeding" includes proceedings in which a custody determination is one of several issues, such as a proceeding for dissolution of marriage or for legal separation of the parties, and includes child neglect and dependency proceedings.

(d) "Decree" or "custody decree" means a custody determination contained in a judicial decree or order made in a custody proceeding, and includes an initial decree and a modification decree.

(e) "Home state" means the state in which the child immediately preceding the time involved lived with the child's parents, a parent, or a person acting as parent, for at least six consecutive months, and in the case of a child less than six months old the state in which the child lived from birth with any of the persons mentioned. Periods of temporary absence of any of the named persons are counted as part of the six-month or other period.

(f) "Initial decree" means the first custody decree concerning a particular child.

(g) "Modification decree" means a custody decree which modifies or replaces a prior decree, whether made by the court which rendered the prior decree or by another court.

(h) "Physical custody" means actual possession and control of a child.

(i) "Person acting as parent" means a person, other than a parent, who has physical custody of a child and who has either been awarded custody by the court or claims a right to custody.

(j) "State" means any state, territory, or possession of the United States, the Commonwealth of Puerto Rico, and the District of Columbia.

3403. (a) A court of this state which is competent to decide child custody matters has jurisdiction to make a child custody determination by initial or modification decree if the conditions as set forth in any of the following paragraphs are met:
    (1) This state (A) is the home state of the child at the time of commencement of the proceeding, or (B) had been the child's home state within six months before commencement of the proceeding and the child is absent from this state because of removal or retention by a person claiming custody of the child or for other reasons, and a parent or person acting as parent continues to live in this state.
    (2) It is in the best interest of the child that a court of this state assume jurisdiction because (A) the child and the child's parents, or the child and at least one contestant, have a significant connection with this state, and (B) there is available in this state substantial evidence concerning the child's present or future care, protection, training, and personal relationships.
    (3) The child is physically present in this state and (A) the child has been abandoned or (B) it is necessary in an emergency to protect the child because the child has been subjected to or threatened with mistreatment or abuse or is otherwise neglected or dependent. For the purposes of this subdivision, "subjected to or threatened with mistreatment or abuse" includes a child who has a parent who is a victim of domestic violence, as defined in Section 6211.
    (4) Both of the following conditions are satisfied:
        (A) It appears that no other state would have jurisdiction under prerequisites substantially in accordance with paragraph (1), (2), or (3) or another state has declined to exercise jurisdiction on the ground that this state is the more appropriate forum to determine the custody of the child.
        (B) It is in the best interest of the child that this court assume jurisdiction.

(b) Except under the conditions specified in paragraphs (3) and (4) of subdivision (a), physical presence in this state of the child, or of the child and one of the contestants, is not alone sufficient to confer jurisdiction on a court of this state to make a child custody determination.

(c) Physical presence of the child, while desirable, is not a prerequisite for jurisdiction to determine the custody of the child.

3404. Before making a decree under this part, reasonable notice and opportunity to be heard shall be given to the contestants, any parent whose parental rights have not been previously terminated, and any person who has physical custody of the child. If any of these persons is outside this state, notice and opportunity to be heard shall be given pursuant to Section 3405.

3405. (a) Notice required for the exercise of jurisdiction over a person outside this state shall be given in a manner reasonably calculated to give actual notice, and may be made in any of the following ways:

(1) By personal delivery outside this state in the manner prescribed for service of process within this state.

(2) In the manner prescribed by the law of the place in which the service is made for service of process in that place in an action in any of its courts of general jurisdiction.

(3) By any form of mail addressed to the person to be served and requesting a receipt.

(4) As directed by the court (including publication, if other means of notification are ineffective).

(b) Notice under this section shall be served, mailed, delivered, or last published at least 10 days before any hearing in this state.

(c) Proof of service outside this state may be made by affidavit of the individual who made the service, or in the manner prescribed by the law of this state, the order pursuant to which the service is made, or the law of the place in which the service is made. If service is made by mail, proof may be a receipt signed by the addressee or other evidence of delivery to the addressee.

(d) Notice is not required if a person submits to the jurisdiction of the court.

3406. (a) A court of this state shall not exercise its jurisdiction under this part if at the time of filing the petition a proceeding concerning the custody of the child was pending in a court of another state exercising jurisdiction substantially in conformity with this part, unless the proceeding is stayed by the court of the other state because this state is a more appropriate forum or for other reasons.

(b) Before hearing the petition in a custody proceeding, the court shall examine the pleadings and other information supplied by the parties under Section 3410 and shall consult the child custody registry established under Section 3417 concerning the pendency of proceedings with respect to the child in other states. If the court has reason to believe that proceedings may be pending in another state, it shall direct an inquiry to the state court administrator or other appropriate official of the other state.

(c) If the court is informed during the course of the proceeding that a proceeding concerning the custody of the child was pending in another state before the court assumed jurisdiction, it shall stay the proceeding and communicate with the court in which the other proceeding is pending to the end that the issue may be litigated in the more appropriate forum and that information be exchanged in accordance with Sections 3420 to 3423, inclusive. If a court of this state has made a custody decree before being informed of a pending proceeding in a court of another state, it shall immediately inform that court of the fact. If the court is informed that a proceeding was commenced in another state after it assumed jurisdiction, it shall likewise inform the other court to the end that the issues may be litigated in the more appropriate forum.

3407. (a) A court which has jurisdiction under this part to make an initial or modification decree may decline to exercise its jurisdiction any time before making a decree if it finds that it is an inconvenient forum to make a custody determination under the circumstances of the case and that a court of another state is a more appropriate forum.

(b) A finding of inconvenient forum may be made upon the court's own motion or upon motion of a party or a guardian ad litem or other representative of the child.

(c) In determining if it is an inconvenient forum, the court shall consider if it is in the interest of the child that another state assume jurisdiction. For this purpose it may take into account the following factors, among others:
(1) If another state is or recently was the child's home state.
(2) If another state has a closer connection with the child and the child's family or with the child and one or more of the contestants.
(3) If substantial evidence concerning the child's present or future care, protection, training, and personal relationships is more readily available in another state.
(4) If the parties have agreed on another forum which is no less appropriate.
(5) If the exercise of jurisdiction by a court of this state would contravene any of the purposes stated in Section 3401.

(d) Before determining whether to decline or retain jurisdiction, the court may communicate with a court of another state and exchange information pertinent to the assumption of jurisdiction by either court with a view to ensuring that jurisdiction will be exercised by the more appropriate court and that a forum will be available to the parties.

(e) If the court finds that it is an inconvenient forum and that a court of another state is a more appropriate forum, it may dismiss the proceedings, or it may stay the proceedings upon condition that a custody proceeding be promptly commenced in another named state or upon any other conditions which may be just and proper, including the condition that a moving party stipulate consent and submission to the jurisdiction of the other forum.

(f) The court may decline to exercise its jurisdiction under this part if a custody determination is incidental to an action for divorce or another proceeding while retaining jurisdiction over the divorce or other proceeding.

(g) If it appears to the court that it is clearly an inappropriate forum, the court may require the party who commenced the proceedings to pay, in addition to the costs of the proceedings in this state, necessary travel and other expenses, including attorney's fees, incurred by other parties or their witnesses. Payment is to be made to the clerk of the court for remittance to the proper party.

(h) Upon dismissal or stay of proceedings under this section, the court shall inform the court found to be the more appropriate forum of this fact, or if the court which would have jurisdiction in the other state is not certainly known, shall transmit the information to the court administrator or other appropriate official for forwarding to the appropriate court.

(i) Any communication received from another state informing this state of a finding of inconvenient forum because a court of this state is the more appropriate forum shall be filed in the custody registry of the appropriate court. Upon assuming jurisdiction, the court of this state shall inform the original court of this fact.

3408. (a) If the petitioner for an initial decree has wrongfully taken the child from another state or has engaged in similar reprehensible conduct, the court may decline to exercise jurisdiction for purposes of adjudication of custody if this is just and proper under the circumstances.

(b) Unless required in the interest of the child, the court shall not exercise its jurisdiction to modify a custody decree of another state if the petitioner, without consent of the person entitled to custody, has improperly removed the child from the physical custody of the person entitled to custody or has improperly retained the child after a visit or other temporary relinquishment of physical custody. If the petitioner has violated any other provision of a custody decree of another state, the court may decline to exercise its jurisdiction if this is just and proper under the circumstances.

(c) Where the court declines to exercise jurisdiction upon petition for an initial custody decree pursuant to subdivision (a), the court shall notify the parent or other appropriate person and the prosecuting attorney of the appropriate jurisdiction in the other state. If a request to that effect is received from the other state, the court shall order the petitioner to appear with the child in a custody proceeding instituted in the other state in accordance with Section 3421. If no request is made within a reasonable time after the notification, the court may entertain a petition to determine custody by the petitioner if it has jurisdiction pursuant to Section 3403.

(d) Where the court refuses to assume jurisdiction to modify the custody decree of another state pursuant to subdivision (b) or pursuant to Section 3414, the court shall notify the person who has legal custody under the decree of the other state and the prosecuting attorney of the appropriate jurisdiction in the other state and may order the petitioner to return the child to the person who has legal custody. If it appears that the order will be ineffective and the legal custodian is ready to receive the child within a period of a few days, the court may place the child in a foster care home for that period, pending return of the child to the legal custodian. At the same time, the court shall advise the petitioner that any petition for modification of custody must be directed to (1) the appropriate court of the other state which has continuing jurisdiction or (2) if that court declines jurisdiction, to a court in a state which has jurisdiction pursuant to Section 3403.

(e) In appropriate cases, a court dismissing a petition under this section may charge the petitioner with necessary travel and other expenses, including attorney's fees and the cost of returning the child to another state.

(f) In making a determination pursuant to subdivisions (a) to (e), inclusive, the court shall not consider as a factor weighing against the petitioner any taking of the child, or retention of the child after a visit or other temporary relinquishment of physical custody, from the person who has legal custody, if there is evidence that the taking or retention of the child was a result of domestic violence against the petitioner, as defined in Section 6211.

3409. (a) Every party in a custody proceeding in the party's first pleading or in an affidavit attached to that pleading shall give information under oath as to the child's present address, the places where the child has lived within the last five years, and the names and present addresses of the persons with whom the child has lived during that period. However, where there are allegations of domestic violence or child abuse, any addresses of the party alleging abuse and of the child that are unknown to the other party are confidential and may not be disclosed in the pleading or affidavit. In this pleading or affidavit, every party shall further declare under oath as to each of the following whether the party:

(1) Has participated, as a party, witness, or in any other capacity, in any other litigation concerning the custody of the same child in this or any other state.

(2) Has information of any custody proceeding concerning the child pending in a court of this or any other state.

(3) Knows of any person not a party to the proceedings who has physical custody of the child or claims to have custody or visitation rights with respect to the child.

(b) If the declaration as to any of the above items is in the affirmative, the declarant shall give additional information under oath as required by the court. The court may examine the parties under oath as to details of the information furnished and as to other matters pertinent to the court's jurisdiction and the disposition of the case.

(c) Each party has a continuing duty to inform the court of any custody proceeding concerning the child in this or any other state of which the party obtained information during this proceeding.

3410. If the court learns from information furnished by the parties pursuant to Section 3409 or from other sources that a person not a party to the custody proceeding has physical custody of the child or claims to have custody or visitation rights with respect to the child, it shall order that person to be joined as a party and to be duly notified of the pendency of the proceeding and of the person's joinder as a party. If the person joined as a party is outside this state, the person shall be served with process or otherwise notified in accordance with Section 3405.

3411. (a) The court may order any party to the proceeding who is within or without this state to appear personally before the court. If that party has physical custody of the child, the court may order him or her to appear personally with the child. If the party who is ordered to appear with the child cannot be served or fails to obey the order, or it appears the order will be ineffective, the court may issue a warrant of arrest against the party and a protective custody warrant for the child, to secure the party's or the child's appearance or both, before the court. The protective custody warrant for the child shall contain an order that the arresting agency shall place the child in protective custody, or return the child as directed by the court. The protective custody warrant may be served in any county in the same manner as a warrant of arrest and may be served at any time of the day or night.

(b) If a party to the proceeding whose presence is desired by the court is outside this state with or without the child the court may order that the notice given under Section 3405 include a statement directing that party to appear personally with or without the child and stating that failure to appear may result in a decision adverse to that party and the issuance of a warrant pursuant to subdivision (a).

(c) If a party to the proceeding who is outside this state is directed to appear under subdivision (b) or desires to appear personally before the court with or without the child, the court may require another party to pay to the clerk of the court travel and other necessary expenses of the party so appearing and of the child if this is just and proper under the circumstances.

3412. A custody decree rendered by a court of this state which had jurisdiction under Section 3403 binds all parties who have been served in this state or notified in accordance with Section 3405 or who have submitted to the jurisdiction of the court, and who have been given an opportunity to be heard. As to these parties, the custody decree is conclusive as to all issues of law and fact decided and as to the custody determination made unless and until that determination is modified pursuant to law, including this part.

3413. The courts of this state shall recognize and enforce an initial or modification decree of a court of another state which had assumed jurisdiction under statutory provisions substantially in accordance with this part or which was made under factual circumstances meeting the jurisdictional standards of this part, so long as this decree has not been modified in accordance with jurisdictional standards substantially similar to those of this part.

3414. (a) If a court of another state has made a custody decree, a court of this state shall not modify that decree unless (1) it appears to the court of this state that the court which rendered the decree does not now have jurisdiction under jurisdictional prerequisites substantially in accordance with this part or has declined to assume jurisdiction to modify the decree and (2) the court of this state has jurisdiction.

(b) If a court of this state is authorized under subdivision (a) and Section 3408 to modify a custody decree of another state, the court shall give due consideration to the transcript of the record and other documents of all previous proceedings submitted to it in accordance with Section 3423.

3415. Section 3140 is applicable to proceedings pursuant to this part.

3416. (a) A certified copy of a custody decree of another state may be filed in the office of the clerk of any superior court of this state. The clerk shall treat the decree in the same manner as a custody decree of the superior court of this state. A custody decree so filed has the same effect and shall be enforced in like manner as a custody decree rendered by a court of this state.

(b) A person violating a custody decree of another state which makes it necessary to enforce the decree in this state may be required to pay necessary travel and other expenses, including attorney's fees, incurred by the party entitled to the custody or that party's witnesses.

3417. The clerk of each superior court shall maintain a registry in which the clerk shall enter all of the following:
    (a) Certified copies of custody decrees of other states received for filing.
    (b) Communications as to the pendency of custody proceedings in other states.
    (c) Communications concerning a finding of inconvenient forum by a court of another state.
    (d) Other communications or documents concerning custody proceedings in another state which may affect the jurisdiction of a court of this state or the disposition to be made by it in a custody proceeding.
    (e) Any custody agreement for which an order is requested regarding a child who is not the subject of another order. The parties shall submit the affidavit required by Section 3409, on the form developed by the Judicial Council for use with Section 3409.

3418. The clerk of a superior court of this state, at the request of the court of another state or at the request of any person who is affected by or has a legitimate interest in a custody decree, shall certify and forward a copy of the decree to that court or person.

3419. In addition to other procedural devices available to a party, any party to the proceeding or a guardian ad litem or other representative of the child may adduce testimony of witnesses, including parties and the child, by deposition or otherwise, in another state. The court on its own motion may direct that the testimony of a person be taken in another state and may prescribe the manner in which and the terms upon which the testimony shall be taken.

3420. (a) A court of this state may request the appropriate court of another state to hold a hearing to adduce evidence, to order a party to produce or give evidence under other procedures of that state, or to have social studies made with respect to the custody of a child involved in proceedings pending in the court of this state; and to forward to the court of this state certified copies of the transcript of the record of the hearing, the evidence otherwise adduced, or any social studies prepared in compliance with the request. The cost of the services may be assessed against the parties or, if necessary, ordered paid by the state.

(b) A court of this state may request the appropriate court of another state to order a party to custody proceedings pending in the court of this state to appear in the proceedings, and if that party has physical custody of the child, to appear with the child. The request may state that travel and other necessary expenses of the party and of the child whose appearance is desired will be assessed against another party or will otherwise be paid.

3421. (a) Upon request of the court of another state, the courts of this state which are competent to hear custody matters may order a person in this state to appear at a hearing to adduce evidence or to produce or give evidence under other procedures available in this state. A certified copy of the transcript of the record of the hearing or the evidence otherwise adduced shall be forwarded by the clerk of the court to the requesting court.

(b) A person within this state may voluntarily give his or her testimony or statement in this state for use in a custody proceeding outside this state.

(c) Upon request of the court of another state, a competent court of this state may order a person in this state to appear alone or with the child in a custody proceeding in another state. The court may condition compliance with the request upon assurance by the other state that travel and other necessary expenses will be advanced or reimbursed. If the person who has physical custody of the child cannot be served or fails to obey the order, or it appears the order will be ineffective, the court may issue a warrant of arrest against the person to secure the person's appearance with the child in the other state.

3422. In any custody proceeding in this state, the court shall preserve the pleadings, orders and decrees, any record that has been made of its hearings, social studies, and other pertinent documents until the child reaches 18 years of age. Upon appropriate request of the court of another state, the court shall forward to the other court certified copies of any or all of such documents.

3423. If a custody decree has been rendered in another state concerning a child involved in a custody proceeding pending in a court of this state, the court of this state upon taking jurisdiction of the case shall request of the court of the other state a certified copy of the transcript of any court record and other documents mentioned in Section 3422.

3424. The general policies of this part extend to the international area. The provisions of this part relating to the recognition and enforcement of custody decrees of other states apply to custody decrees and decrees involving legal institutions similar in nature to custody rendered by appropriate authorities of other nations if reasonable notice and opportunity to be heard were given to all affected persons.

3425. Upon the request of a party to a custody proceeding which raises a question of existence or exercise of jurisdiction under this part, the case shall be given calendar priority and handled expeditiously.

# THE PARENTAL KIDNAPPING PREVENTION ACT

*As Adopted by the State of Wyoming*

## 28 USC Sec. 1738A

Sec. 1738A. Full faith and credit given to child custody determinations

(a) The appropriate authorities of every State shall enforce according to its terms, and shall not modify except as provided in subsection (f) of this section, any child custody determination made consistently with the provisions of this section by a court of another State.

(b) As used in this section, the term—

    (1) "child" means a person under the age of eighteen;

    (2) "contestant" means a person, including a parent, who claims a right to custody or visitation of a child;

    (3) "custody determination" means a judgment, decree, or other order of a court providing for the custody or visitation of a child, and includes permanent and temporary orders, and initial orders and modifications;

    (4) "home State" means the State in which, immediately preceding the time involved, the child lived with his parents, a parent, or a person acting as parent, for at least six consecutive months, and in the case of a child less than six months old, the State in which the child lived from birth with any of such persons. Periods of temporary absence of any of such persons are counted as part of the six-month or other period;

    (5) "modification" and "modify" refer to a custody determination which modifies, replaces, supersedes, or otherwise is made subsequent to, a prior custody determination concerning the same child, whether made by the same court or not;

(6) "person acting as a parent" means a person, other than a parent, who has physical custody of a child and who has either been awarded custody by a court or claims a right to custody;

(7) "physical custody" means actual possession and control of a child; and

(8) "State" means a State of the United States, the District of Columbia, the Commonwealth of Puerto Rico, or a territory or possession of the United States.

(c) A child custody determination made by a court of a State is consistent with the provisions of this section only if—

(1) such court has jurisdiction under the law of such State; and

(2) one of the following conditions is met:

(A) such State (i) is the home State of the child on the date of the commencement of the proceeding, or (ii) had been the child's home State within six months before the date of the commencement of the proceeding and the child is absent from such State because of his removal or retention by a contestant or for other reasons, and a contestant continues to live in such State;

(B)(i) it appears that no other State would have jurisdiction under subparagraph (A), and (ii) it is in the best interest of the child that a court of such State assume jurisdiction because (I) the child and his parents, or the child and at least one contestant, have a significant connection with such State other than mere physical presence in such State, and (II) there is available in such State substantial evidence concerning the child's present or future care, protection, training, and personal relationships;

(C) the child is physically present in such State and (i) the child has been abandoned, or (ii) it is necessary in an emergency to protect the child because he has been subjected to or threatened with mistreatment or abuse;

(D)(i) it appears that no other State would have jurisdiction under subparagraph (A), (B), (C), or (E), or another State has declined to exercise jurisdiction on the ground that the State whose jurisdiction is in issue is the more appropriate forum to determine the custody of the child, and (ii) it is in the best interest of the child that such court assume jurisdiction; or

(E) the court has continuing jurisdiction pursuant to subsection (d) of this section.

(d) The jurisdiction of a court of a State which has made a child custody determination consistently with the provisions of this section continues as long as the requirement of subsection (c)(1) of this section continues to be met and such State remains the residence of the child or of any contestant.

(e) Before a child custody determination is made, reasonable notice and opportunity to be heard shall be given to the contestants, any parent whose parental rights have not been previously terminated and any person who has physical custody of a child.

(f) A court of a State may modify a determination of the custody of the same child made by a court of another State, if—

(1) it has jurisdiction to make such a child custody determination; and

(2) the court of the other State no longer has jurisdiction, or it has declined to exercise such jurisdiction to modify such determination.

(g) A court of a State shall not exercise jurisdiction in any proceeding for a custody determination commenced during the pendency of a proceeding in a court of another State where such court of that other State is exercising jurisdiction consistently with the provisions of this section to make a custody determination.

# INDEX

## Books from Allworth Press

**The Retirement Handbook: How to Maximize Your Assets and Protect Your Quality of Life** by Carl W. Battle (softcover, 6 × 9, 256 pages, $18.95)

**Your Living Trust and Estate Plan: How to Maximize Your Family's Assets and Protect Your Loved Ones** by Harvey J. Platt (softcover, 6 × 9, 256 pages, $14.95)

**The Patent Guide: A Friendly Guide to Protecting and Profiting from Patents** by Carl W. Battle (softcover, 6 × 9, 224 pages, $18.95)

**The Copyright Guide: A Friendly Guide for Protecting and Profiting from Copyrights** by Lee Wilson (softcover, 6 × 9, 192 pages, $18.95)

**Legal-Wise: Self-Help Legal Guide for Everyone, Third Edition** by Carl W. Battle (softcover, 8½ × 11, 208 pages, $18.95)

**Retire Smart** by David and Virginia Cleary (softcover, 6 × 9, 224 pages, $12.95)

**Hers: The Wise Woman's Guide to Starting a Business on $2,000 or Less, Revised Edition** by Carol Milano (softcover, 6 × 9, 192 pages, $16.95)

**Immigration Questions and Answers, Revised Edition** by Carl R. Baldwin (softcover, 6 × 9, 182 pages, $14.95)

**The Law (In Plain English)® for Small Businesses, Third Edition** by Leonard DuBoff (softcover, 6 × 9, 256 pages, $19.95)

**The Secret Life of Money: How Money Can Be Food for the Soul** by Tad Crawford (softcover, 5½ × 8½, 304 pages, $14.95)

**Old Money: The Mythology of Wealth in America** by Nelson W. Aldrich, Jr. (softcover, 6 × 9, 340 pages, $16.95)

**Once in Golconda: A True Drama of Wall Street 1920–1938** by John Brooks, Introduction by Tad Crawford (hardcover, 5½ × 8½, 320 pages, $21.95)

**The Go-Go Years: The Drama and Crashing Finale of Wall Street's Bullish 60s** by John Brooks (hardcover, 6 × 9, 392 pages, $24.95)

Please write to request our free catalog. To order by credit card, call 1-800-491-2808 or send a check or money order to Allworth Press, 10 East 23rd Street, Suite 210, New York, NY 10010. Include $5 for shipping and handling for the first book ordered and $1 for each additional book. Ten dollars plus $1 for each additional book if ordering from Canada. New York State residents must add sales tax.

If you would like to see our complete catalog on the World Wide Web, you can find us at *www.allworth.com*.